The Bible Study Tool Box

A STUDY MANUAL ON BIBLICAL HERMENEUTICS

The Bible Study Tool Box

A STUDY MANUAL ON BIBLICAL HERMENEUTICS

DR. DANIEL S. HAIFLEY

*I would like to dedicate this book to
My father, Dr. David R. Haifley,
Who taught the Word of God faithfully
for over forty years,
And began teaching me these basic
Principles when I was a child.*

Acknowledgements

Special recognition should be made to Dr. Mark Cambron, who was my father's teacher. He provided me with a base to work from in his writings on this subject.

This is a good opportunity to thank Dr. Steven Hite for encouragement and assistance in developing this text, and Bob Yoder for helping with the design.

I would also like to thank Abigail Mitchell and Lois Rees, and Dori Douglass for assisting in the original proofreading of the text,.

To my friends at the Grace Bible Baptist Church of New Paris, IN and Maranatha Baptist Church of Mattoon, IL for providing the opportunity to study, write and publish: Thank you from the bottom of my heart.

And to my wife Elizabeth I owe an eternal debt of gratitude for her faithful support and counsel.

Sincerely,
Daniel S. Haifley, Th.D., D.D.
November 6, 2013

Preface

While this can not be called an exhaustive work on the subject of hermeneutics, it is a tool box designed for the average Bible student. The intent is to provide the layman with the tools to unravel the most intense theological tangles. I do not claim this material as entirely original. It is built upon generations of Bible scholars who have assembled tools to help us in understanding the words of God in the Word of God.

Understanding the Bible can be like assembling a puzzle. Each generation lays down its pieces, and then the next generation lays down its pieces. In this way, building upon the study of previous generations, the overall picture of God's truth becomes more clear than ever before.

Study this text, add to it your own findings, keeping in mind that the generations after you are building on your discoveries.

Contents

Acknowledgements.. 6

Preface 7

Introduction 11

1. The Framework Principle 17

2. The Unity Principle 25

....*The Christo-centric Principle pg. 28*

3. The Context Principle 31

4. The Dispensation Principle 49

5. The Covenant Principle 55

6. The Ethnic Principle 71

7. The Agreement Principle 79

8. The Direct Statement Principle 87

9. The First Mention Principle 97

10. The Subsequent Mention Principle 109

11. The Full Mention Principle 113

12. The Application Principle 119

13. The Consequence Principle 127

14. The Principles of Prophecy 133

15. The Divine Will in Revelation Principle 139

16. The Human Willingness Principle 143

17. The Progressive Revelation Principle 147

18. The Illustrative Principle 153

19. The Law of Repetition Principle 157

20. The Numerical Principle 161

21. The Principle of Types 169

22. The Gap Principle 175

23. The Discrimination Principle 185

Appendix "A" 189

Appendix "B" 191

Appendix "C" 195

Appendix "D" 197

Appendix "E" 203

References 207

It shall greatly help ye to understand
Scripture
If thou mark,
Not only what is spoken or written,
But of whom,
And to whom,
With what words,
At what time,
Where,
To what intent,
With what circumstances,
Considering what goeth before
And what followeth.

John Wycliffe

Introduction to
<u>The Study of the Bible</u>

- Hermeneutics
  –the science of Biblical interpretation
- God's will is for us to learn.
- Study is necessary for us to grow in Christ.
- The Word of God is the most powerful tool.

Introduction to
the Study of the Bible

*"**Study** to shew thyself approved unto God,
a workman that needeth not to be ashamed,
rightly dividing the word of truth."*
II Timothy 2:15

In simple terms, hermeneutics is a study of how to interpret God's Word. By its proper definition, it is the *science* of Biblical interpretation. Science is defined as *a branch of knowledge conducted on objective principles involving the systemized observation of and experiment with phenomena of a specialized type or on a specified subject. Since God created the laws that govern scientific principles it would also stand to reason that God would apply the same characteristics of science to His Word. As algebra has postulates and theorems, the Bible has principles, covenants, and

> ## *Hermeneutics*
>
> *The science
> and art of
> Biblical
> interpretation*

*Readers Digest Oxford Complete Wordfinder © 1996 Oxford University Press

dispensations. This book will discuss those principles and how to apply them so that the layman can fully immerse himself in the vast riches of the Bible *"rightly dividing the word of truth."*

God is adamant about His people learning about Him. As Hosea points out, it is for our own good.

> *"My people are destroyed for a lack*
> *of knowledge: because thou hast*
> *rejected knowledge, I will also reject thee,"*
> Hosea 4:6

We will self-destruct without an understanding of the Scriptures. In fact it is that consistent Bible study that will build us into what God intends for us to be.

II Peter 1:2-8 shows us that the knowledge of God (brought about by the study of the Word of God) gives us all things that pertain to life and godliness. In other words: to live the Christian life you must have a knowledge of God.

> *"Grace and peace be multiplied unto*
> *you **through the knowledge of God**,*
> *and of Jesus our Lord, According as*
> *his divine power hath given unto us all*
> *things that pertain unto life and godli-*
> *ness, through the knowledge of him*
> *that hath called us to glory and virtue:*
> *Whereby are given unto us exceeding*
> *great and precious promises: that by*

*these ye might be partakers of the divine nature, having escaped the corruption that is in the world through lust......For if these things be in you, and abound, they make you that **ye shall neither be barren nor unfruitful in the knowledge of our Lord Jesus Christ.**" II Peter 1:2-8*

Without study, there is no knowledge; without knowledge of the Lord Jesus Christ, there is barrenness and unfruitfulness. Joshua 1:8 goes on to tell us that true success will only come in our lives if we meditate on the Word of God:

*"**This book of the law** shall not depart out of thy mouth; but thou shalt meditate therein day and night, that thou mayest observe to do according to all that is written therein: for **then thou shalt make thy way prosperous, and then thou shalt have good success.**"*

Although meditating is different than studying, a person cannot meditate on that which he has not studied. The real learning comes when you contemplate on what you have studied.

Let's take a quick look at what Paul told Timothy about the value of scripture. Note the emphasis of the phrase "all scripture." The cost was high for the preservation of each and every word that is in the Bible. That should give us an indication what

God thinks about each word, and therefore we should be careful to study every word that God has provided for us.

> "***All scripture is given*** *by inspiration of God, and is profitable for doctrine, for reproof, for correction, for instruction in righteousness:* ***That the man of God may be perfect, throughly furnished*** *unto all good works.*"
>   *II Timothy 3:16-17*

Someone once explained these verses this way:
- Doctrine is "what is right"
- Reproof is "what is not right"
- Correction is "how to get right"
- Instruction is "how to stay right"

In addition to these very good definitions the casual observer should notice the fact that the study of the Word of God is necessary:
- To perfect the man of God
- To furnish the man of God
- To enable the man of God to do good works

The consequence for not being a good student of the Book is found in Hebrews 5:12-14 which states that if one does not study the Bible, he is a baby in the faith and will always remain so.

The Word of God is the tool that formed the world (Psalm 33:6). The Word of God is the tool that brings new birth (Romans 1:16). The Word of God is the tool that washes impurities from our lives (Ephesians 5:26). The Word of God is the tool that builds faith (Romans 10:17). God has given the Christian workman this tool to use, and He has commanded us to study it—to learn to use it– to understand it.

Verses for further study:

Psalms 1, Romans 1:16, Romans 10:17, II Timothy 3:15, Ephesians 6:17, John 16:13, and Colossians 3:16.

The Framework Principle

- The Divisions of the Book
    a. The Old Testament
        1. Books of Moses
        2. Books of History
        3. Books of Poetry
        4. Books of Prophecy
    b. The New Testament
        1. Historical Books
        2. Doctrinal Books
        3. Prophetical Book

- The Titles of the Book
    a. The Bible
    b. The Word of God
    c. The Scriptures
    d. The Testaments
    e. The Oracles
    f. The Holy Writ
    g. The Cannon

chapter ONE

The Framework Principle

For the prophecy came not in old time by the will of man: but holy men of God spake as they were moved by the Holy Ghost.
2 Peter 1:21

The Old Testament Scriptures have been handed down to us through many generations of Jewish scribes. They were meticulous in their care to preserve the scrolls and to copy accurately. We owe them for most of the divisions in the Old Testament. See Romans 3:1-2.

The New Testament was assembled into one volume by many scholars (one of the most notable being Erasmus of Rotterdam) from thousands of letters sent to churches and copied and recopied over the centuries. Finally the burden was placed upon certain men who began a steady stream of translation work into the English language.

The Bible was written by 40 different men over a period of about 4,000 years

In the process of the translation work it became necessary to identify passages of scripture for referencing and comparison. Therefore these men of God devised a plan to include chapters and verses in the texts which had originally been written in paragraph form. These chapter and verse divisions are not necessarily inspired and can sometimes confuse the meaning of the text by breaking the flow of a specific line of thought. However, they are quite useful for a detailed study of the Scripture, and have generally been accepted in every language and every translation to date.

.—The Divisions of the Book

a. The Old Testament
  (1) The Books of Moses (The Law)
     Genesis - Deuteronomy
  (2) The Books of History
     Joshua – Esther
  (3) The Books of Poetry
     Job – Song of Solomon,* Lamentations
  (4) The Books of Prophecy
     There are two ways scholars divide the Books of Prophecy. The Traditional Division is usually taught in Sunday School and is an easy frame of reference. It is based upon the Jewish scrolls. The major prophets each have their own scrolls. The minor prophets are compiled together in one scroll. However, a more Scientific Division

---

*The Song of Solomon is also called "The Canticles." The Strong's Concordance uses this designation.

introduced by C.I. Schofield is based upon when the prophets actually lived and wrote. It gives the Bible student a good background into the why's and wherefore's of the prophets' message. The Pre-exilic prophets preached during the era before the great Babylonian exile of the Jews. The Exilic prophets preached during the Babylonian exile, and the Post-exilic prophets preached after the Babylonian exile.

Traditional Division:
(a) Major Prophets
Isaiah – Daniel
(b) Minor Prophets
Hosea – Malachi
Scientific Division:
(a) **Pre-Exilic Prophets**
Isaiah, Micah, Nahum, Jonah, Amos, Hosea, Habakkuk, Zephaniah, Jeremiah, Joel, Obadiah
(b) **Exilic Prophets**
Ezekiel, Daniel, Jeremiah
(c) **Post-Exilic Prophets**
Haggai, Zechariah, Malachi

Synoptic Traits

Portrayals of Jesus

Mathew—King

Mark—Servant

Luke—Son of Man

John—Son of God

b. The New Testament
(1) The Historical Books
(a) **The Gospels**
Each one of the Gospels presents Christ from a different perspective.

Bible Labels

- *Bible*
- *Word of God*
- *Scriptures*
- *Testaments*
- *Oracles*
- *Holy Writ*
- *Canon*

- **Matthew**—*As King of the Jews*

This book was written by Matthew, also called Levi, who had once been a tax collector. Matt. 9:9-13, Luke 5:27-29.

- **Mark**—*As a Servant*

Another name for this man was John Mark. We find more about him by reading Acts 13:5, Acts 15:36-41, II Timothy 4:11. Mark's Gospel seems to be aimed at the Gentile believers, and leaves out much of the Jewish contexts found in the other Gospels.

- **Luke**—*As the Son of Man*

Luke is called "The Beloved Physician" by the Apostle Paul and was one of Paul's traveling companions. Acts is part two of Luke's Gospel.

- **John**—*As the Son of God*

John seemed to have a closer relationship to Christ than the others hence a more clear understanding of His deity of Christ. John refers to himself as the one "whom Jesus loved."

(b) **Acts**

Its full name, "The Acts of the Apostles," describes the content of the book.

(2) The Doctrinal Books
(a) Pauline Epistles

These were letters written by the Apostle Paul.

- Romans - Hebrews*

(b) General Epistles

Each one of these Epistles are written by the one whose name they carry.

- James

James was the pastor of the church of Jerusalem (Acts 15). Although its contents are definitely for the Church as a whole, he directed his arguments more towards the Jewish believers.

- I & II Peter

Peter's epistles following immediately on the heels of James was in contrast directed to the Gentile believers.

- I John

This book is one of the most intimate books in the New Testament. It has been suggested that it was designed for John's own children, because of his often statement "my little children." However, there is no way to know this for sure.

- II & III John

These are short notes written to individuals, the first written to the "Elect Lady." This could be John's wife, or it could be a reference to Mary, the mother of Jesus. III John is written to Gaius.

---

*There is some difference of opinion as to the writing of the book of Hebrews. This author believes that Paul was the author of the book. Some have pointed out that it contains a slightly different writing style than what Paul was accustomed to using in his other epistles. It is important to remember that it is a theological dissertation presented to Paul's own people. You will find a more refined presentation in Hebrews for that reason, but it is still marked with the same kind of phrasing found in his other letters.

- Jude
Jude writes concerning the apostasy.

(3) The Prophetical Book
- Revelation
-The Titles of the Book

a. *The Bible*
The most common name. It comes from the Greek "τα βιβλια" *(ta biblia)* which means "the books." Psalm 40:7, Hebrews 10:7
b. *The Word of God*
This is a reference to the individual words of God as well as the collective word. John 3:34. Revelation 17:17, Hebrews 4:12
c. *The Scriptures*
This comes from the Latin word *scriptura* which means "the writings." I Corinthians 15:1-4, II Peter 3:16, II Timothy 3:15-17
d. *The Testaments*
Usually the testaments are described as the Old Testament and the New Testament. A covenant is another name for a testament. The Bible is referred to in this manner as a reflection of two of God's covenants, Law and Grace. II Corinthians 3:6, II Corinthians 3:14, Hebrews 9:15
e. *The Oracles*
Oracles is also derived from the Latin, *oraculum,* and it means "to speak." It refers primarily to someone speaking who has Great Authority. Romans 3:2, I Peter 4:11
f. *The Holy Writ*

Occasionally you will hear the Bible referred to by this name. The word "writ" is an Anglo-Saxon word which means "a formal writing of any kind." In law a Writ is a precept issued by some court or magistrate in the name of the government. A Writ is issued in pursuance of a decree, judgment, or order of the court.   Nehemiah 9:13-14, Isaiah 28:9-10

g. *Canon*

The word canon has its roots in both the Greek language (κανον) and the Ecclesiastical Latin (*canonicus*). It has several depths of meaning, but in this usage it means "a collection of sacred books accepted as genuine. It should be noted here that there also is a collection of ecclesiastical books that are not considered to be genuine, and they are called "The Apocrypha."

The Unity Principle

I.   The Beginning and the End
     A. The Beginning
     B. The Alpha and The Omega
     C. The Ending

II. The Theme
     A. Introduced
     B. Illustrated
     C. The Climax

III. The Hero of the Story
     A. The Hero Introduced
     B. The Hero Illustrated
     C. The Hero Explained

IV. The Plot
     A. Introduced
     B. God's Interest in Separation
     C. Our Separation

V.   The Conflict
     A. The Climax
     B. The Victor
     C. The Continued Work
     D. The Champion
     E. The Victors
     F. The Judgment
     G. The Promise

chapter *TWO*

The Unity Principle

Then said I, Lo, I come: in the volume of the book
it is written of me, I delight to do thy will,
O my God: yea, thy law is within my heart.
Psalm 40:7-8

The King James Version of the Bible is recognized by literary critics as the "Classic of Classics." It is important to note that the Bible is considered to be one unit, even though it is a collection of writings authored by 40 different men, on 3 different continents spanning approximately 4,000 years.

I. **The Beginning and the End**

> There are actually 66 individual books that make up the Bible. The writer in Psalms (Psalms 40:7-8) and the writer in Hebrews (Hebrews 10:7) referred to them as "the volume." Note that the book of Genesis and the book of Revelation give us a distinct beginning and a distinct ending to the volume.
>
> A. The Beginning Genesis 1:1
> B. The Alpha and the Omega

The Bible
As Classical Literature

Introduction	Main Characters	Hero Introduced
"In the Beginning" Genesis 1:1	The Trinity Genesis 1:1-3 The People Genesis 1:26-28	The Light Genesis 1:3-4

Plot	Problem	Building Conflict
Separation of Light and darkness Genesis 1:4	The People sided with darkness Genesis 3	"Cain joins darkness" "The Flood" The Old Testament

Climax	Denouement	Conclusion
Darkness appears to win, nailing Light to a Cross. Light breaks out of the tomb on the third day. Matthew 27-28	Light is given to the people Acts 2 Revelation 1	Light is the Victor Revelation 21:23

Revelation 1:8,11
C. The Ending   Revelation 22:18-19
The Bible is the final authority.

II. One Theme - Redemption

The entire volume of scripture has a single
thread running through it—the theme of
redemption.
A. Introduced in Genesis 1:2
B. Illustrated
Noah - from a wicked society
Israel - from slavery
Caanan - from wicked people
Lot - from a wicked city
Nineveh - from a wicked lifestyle
C. The Climax
The Crucifixion and Resurrection

III. The Hero of the Story

The Bible has a definite Hero. Jesus Christ is
the Hero of the entire story; however, He
is represented by "Light." You will learn
quite a bit about Him if you find every
place that light is brought into each story.
A. The Hero introduced -The Light
Genesis 1:3
B. The Hero identified John 1:1-12
C. The Hero explained
The rainbow - a promise
Sodom and Gomorrah - judgment
The burning bush - the "I Am"

The pillar of fire - the leader
Elijah's experience - all-powerful

This is sometimes called "The Christo-Centric Principle." (See Appendix A.) It's important to understand that the Mind of God is centered on Christ. All angelic thought and ministry is centered on Christ. All satanic and demonic hatred is centered on Christ. All human hopes are centered on Christ. The whole material universe is centered on Christ. The entire written Word of God is centered on Christ.

IV. The Plot - separation of light and darkness
A. Introduced   Genesis 1:4
B. God has always been interested in the separation of light and darkness
   Ezekiel 22:26 .
C. Our Separation—We are called out
   I Peter 2:9

V. The Conflict – between Light and darkness
A. The conflict between light and darkness
   comes to a climax in   Matthew 27:45
B. The victor appears in   Matthew 28:1-3
C. We find Him continuing his work
   Acts 2:1-3
D. The Champion   Revelation 19:11-16
   Matthew 24:27
E. The Victors Revelation 15:2
F. The Judgment   Revelation 20:15
G. The Promise   Revelation 21:23

The Context Principle

I. The Different Kinds of Contexts
      A. Near Context
      B. Remote Context
      C. Complete Context
      D. Historical Context

II. The Purpose of the Context Principle
      A. To answer difficult questions
      B. To shed light on a particular story
      C. To protect a truth
      D. To define a word

chapter *THREE*

The Context Principle

*"Knowing this first, that no prophecy of the scripture is
of any private interpretation." II Peter 1:20*

This principle has also been called the Comparative Principle and the Parallel Principle. Simply stated, the Context principle reminds us to study each verse, phrase, and word within its context. Without a context, the Bible can be made to say or teach anything.

> *Without a context, the Bible can be made to say anything*

I. The Different Kinds of Contexts
There are four kinds of contexts:
A. Near Context – all of the words and verses surrounding a particular passage give insight as to what circumstances the verse was given.

B. Remote Context – all of the verses in the Bible dealing with a given subject when gathered together can reveal more information collectively than individual verses alone.

C. Complete Context – God's attitude on other issues will sometimes give light on the text in question.

D. Historical Context - the background of the author and of the people being spoken too, including issues and customs of the day.

Here is an example of the four different kinds of contexts using Hebrews 11:5 as the text in question.

"By faith Enoch was translated that he should not see death; and was not found, because God had translated him: for before his translation he had this testimony, that he pleased God." Hebrews 11:5

Near Context of Hebrews 11:5

Hebrews 11:6 – a continuation of the thought
Hebrews 11 – vs. 5 is part of an entire topic

First you look at the near context, ie., all of the verses surrounding this verse. You find first of all that this verse is a partial thought. Verse six continues the thought. Then you will notice that the two verses actually fit into a larger picture.

Remote Context of Hebrews 11:5

Genesis 5:21-24 - the original story
Jude 14-15 – more about Enoch

I Thessalonians 4:13-18 – more about the subject of translation

A search for remote contexts will first take us to the original story in Genesis 5. Then we will look for any other reference to Enoch, the principal person in the verse. It will also be interesting to do a search on the subject of translation.

Complete Context of Hebrews 11:5
Revelation 21:3 – God with us
Matthew 1:23 – God with us

An understanding of why God would even translate anyone will take us through the whole Bible. We will begin to see a pattern of God's desire to be with us.

A verse taken out of the context of the Bible itself is an incomplete thought. The world often does this. A Bible student must remember that the Bible is not a "Toastmaster's Handbook," but it is the power of God (Romans 1:16). Each verse and phrase hold a premium place in the Word of God. Each one points toward the Creator and, in some way, reveals Him to us.

Historical Context of Hebrews 11:5
Matthew 24:37-39 - *As in the days of Noah*

Research into the time in which Enoch lived and preached will help us understand his message and will give us insight into why God translated him.

II. The Purpose of the Context Principle:

A. The Context Principle will answer difficult questions.

Sometimes in the course of Bible Study you will come across some difficult questions. Maybe those questions will have nothing at all to do with doctrine and maybe they will. However, using this context principle you will be able to sort through fact and fiction and possibly come to some refreshing conclusions.

Some time ago I was arrested by the question "When was the book of Job written?" Some try to place his writings in the patriarchal age. Some say he was contemporary with Moses. Still others believe he lived in captivity in Egypt and went through the Exodus. Some put him in the time of the Israelite judges, others in the time of the Babylonian captivity, having been teacher of a school at Tiberias in Palestine, and carried away into Babylon with the rest of his countrymen. Each viewpoint has its perspectives and reasons, but as you can see they are very diverse. So I set about to form an opinion of my own. Using the Context Principle almost exclusively, here are the results which illustrate how you can use this principle to answer difficult questions.

Four Contexts

- *Near*
- *Remote*
- *Complete*
- *Historical*

The Question:
"When was the book of Job written?"

Near Context
First we must look at the near context, that is, starting at the very beginning of the text, find out everything we can about this man. Two things come to light right away.

1. There was a man. Job chapter 1
   This is not a metaphorical story this is about a real man that lived through a very difficult time.
2. He lived in the land of Uz.

Remote Context
Uz is our first clue to the culture and surroundings of Job. So lets follow this lead and see what we find. The Remote Context will take us to every reference that we can find about Uz.

1. The First Uz was a grandson of Shem.
   Genesis 10:23, I Chronicles 1:17

⇒ **1st Deduction** – This eliminates the possibility of these events taking place before the Flood. Job takes place after the Flood.

2. Digging still deeper, we find a second Uz who was a descendant of Esau.
   Genesis 36:28, I Chronicles 1:42
3. We then find a direct reference to the Land of Uz mentioned three times. Notice
   Job 1:1, Jeremiah 25:20,
   Lamentations 4:21

⇒ **2nd Deduction** - Since Lamentations clearly describes Uz as a descendant of Edom, the story must take place after Esau. Another interesting note is that Jeremiah is the only prophet to mention this land. He prophesied in the pre-exilic and the exilic time periods.

    4. Where was this land of Uz? Job 1:3 tells us that he had sheep, camels, oxen and she asses, and that **he was the greatest of all the men of the East.** This sounds a little bit like Abraham. In fact Genesis 25:6 tells us that Abraham sent some of his children to the east country. Genesis 29:1 tells us that Jacob went to find a wife from the "land of the people of the east."

⇒ **3rd Deduction** - It is definitely within the realm of possibility that Job was related to, or a descendant of, Abraham.

Complete Context

Let's go now to the discussion between Satan and God about the hedge. Because this discourse is waged in heaven, the Complete Context is the direction we must go. The Complete Context will help us read between the lines. It goes right to the character of God and the wicked heart of Satan.

    1. Satan claimed that God had made a wall of protection (*hedge*) about Job, which gave Job an edge over everybody else. Of

course, the logical conclusion is that everybody else was not doing as well.
Job 1:9-10

2. Being the father of lies everything Satan says is suspect (Complete Context). God, however, Who knows all things (Complete Context), did not argue with Satan; He removed the hedge only to give the Devil a more even playing field. God's actions seem to give credence to Satan's argument, which leads us to wonder: **What was going on outside of the hedge?** Job 1:12

⇒ **4th Deduction** - If we can find out what might have been happening to everyone else outside of the hedge we might be able to zero in on the time period in which the book was written.

Historical Context

The questions that arose in the last section can be answered simply by looking at what happened to Job as soon as the hedge was removed.

1. The Sabeans attacked
   a. These people are mentioned only three other times in the Bible: Isaiah 45:14, Ezekiel 23:42, and Joel 3:8.
   b. When those prophets preached will give us and idea when the Sabeans were a threat to Israel.
      Ezekiel prophesied during the Babylonian exile.

Isaiah and Joel both prophesied before the Babylonian exile.

Joel's prophecy indicates that the Sabeans were part of the judgment of God on Israel during the exile.

⇒ **5th Deduction** - Our first impression would be that Job should be placed in the same time period as those books who mentioned the Sabeans.

2. The second thing to happen to Job after the hedge was removed, was that the Fire of God fell.

Our first thought would be that this has absolutely nothing to do with the time in which Job lived, but a search through the Bible on the Fire of God reveals a curious "coincidence." There are 40 references to fire in Jeremiah, the book that prophesied of the impending judgment on Israel. Note Jeremiah 4:4, 6:1, 15:14, 17:27, 21:10,12,14.

3. The third thing to happen was that the Chaldeans attacked.

a. Only five books of the Bible mention this group of people.

b. Those five books were written during the same timeframe as the Sabeans.

Isaiah – pre-exilic
(before Babylonian exile)
Habakkuk – pre-exilic

Jeremiah – both pre-exilic and
exilic
Ezekiel – exilic
(during Babylonian exile)
Daniel – exilic

4. The fourth thing to happen was that a great Wind from the wilderness came. Again your first impression would seem to indicate that this would not have anything to do with the time period; however, a closer look in the prophets reveals surprising predictions:

Jeremiah 13:24 *Therefore will I scatter them as the stubble that passeth away by the wind of the wilderness.*

Notice the mention of a destroying wind to come from God as a means of judgment: Jeremiah 4:11-12, 5:13, 10:13, 22:22, 51:1,16

⇒ **6th Deduction** – Given all of this contextual evidence, we must conclude that Job was an individual who lived during the time of the Babylonian exile. He must have been a faithful man surrounded by a culture of wicked Israelites. God's promises from the time of Moses were in effect in his life. The hedge of protection was God's blessing on his life. When the contest with Satan was begun, the hedge was lifted, and Job was exposed to all the curses falling on his countrymen.

B. The Context Principle will shed light on a particular story.

The story of Benaiah in II Sam 23:20-21 raises some questions in our minds. He went against an Egyptian with no more than a staff, and then plucked the Egyptian's spear out of his hand and killed him with his own spear. You have to wonder if the man was crazy or desperate. Why did he not use a normal fighting weapon? A sword for example? To answer this question we should first go to the remote context. Let's find out everything we can about the fighting techniques of the Israelites in those days.

Remote Context

Judges 5:8 - an unarmed army
Judges 3:16 - Ehud made a dagger
Judges 3:31 - Shamgar used an ox goad
Judges 15:15 - Samson used the jawbone
of an ass
I Samuel 13:22 - only Saul and Jonathan
had a sword
I Samuel 17:50 - David used a sling

*see also:*Judges 20:16, I Chronicles 12:2,
II Chronicles 14:8, Psalm 78:9

Historical Context

The Historical Context shows us some interesting facts as well.

1. When tracing the use of swords through the

Bible, you will find that the Israelites were using them up until Judges 21:10. At that point they disappeared in the text until we find Jonathan and Saul with the only swords in Israel (I Sam 13:22).

2. It is in I Samuel 13:19-21 that you will discover the Philistines had made a "weapon control law." No Israelites were allowed to own a weapon. Judges 13:1 reveals that God had delivered Israel into the hand of the Philistines so Israel was at their mercy.

3. It is not until II Chronicles 26:11-15 that the people get back their weapons when King Uzziah outfitted the people with the tools of war.

⇒ **Deduction** - Benaiah simply had no weapon to use against the Egyptians. In fact, nobody did. This gives us an understanding of why the Israelites where hiding from Goliath and why Saul would have given David his armor and sword.

C. The Context Principle will protect a truth.

In the course of your Bible study, you will run across verses that may seem to explain something that is entirely different than what you might understand the Bible to say in another place. By using the Context Principle you can often unravel those difficult questions and come up with a more complete understanding of the subject in question.

For example there is a doctrine of security in Christ that incites much controversy between believers. It has many names: "Security of the Believer," "Eternal Security," "Once saved always saved," "Once in Grace always in Grace." There are some verses that would indicate that this is not a true doctrine. Notice what Hebrews 6:4-6 says:

> *For it is impossible for those who were once enlightened, and have tasted of the heavenly gift, and were made partakers of the Holy Ghost, And have tasted the good word of God, and the powers of the world to come, If they shall fall away, to renew them again unto repentance; seeing they crucify to themselves the Son of God afresh, and put him to an open shame.*

The earnest student should not accept a doctrine just because that is what he was taught. Instead, he should be as the noble Bereans of Acts 17 and search the scriptures to find out what God has to say.

Remote Context
An honest search will find other references to *falling away* that seem to be similar to the one in Hebrews. These verses should be studied with care.
* Having to do with *falling away*:
    1 Timothy 4:1 – Depart from the faith
    II Thessalonians 2:3 - Falling away
    II Peter 2:19-22 – The sow returns

Turning now to the other side of the question, let's find the verses that would indicate that salvation is eternal and cannot be lost.

- Having to do with eternal salvation:
  John 3:16, John 10:27-28, I Peter 1:23, John 3:36, John 6:37, Romans 8:38-39, I John 5:13, Romans 8:1, Hebrews 10:14, II Corinthians 5:17, Hebrews 10:17, Romans 10:13, John 14:6, Psalms 103:12, John 3:15, II Timothy 2:13, Romans 8:35-37, Romans 11:29, Revelation 3:5, Micah 7:19, Ephesians 4:30, Philippians 1:6, Philippians 1:21, John 4:13-14, Romans 6:23, I Peter 1:4, John 3:18, John 5:24, John 20:31, I John 5:11-12, Psalms 23:6, I Peter 1:5, Galatians 2:20, II Corinthians 5:21, Romans 10:9-10, Romans 5:1, Titus 1:2, II Corinthians 5:1, II Timothy 1:12, Romans 8:31, Romans 8:33, Romans 9:33, I John 1:5, I John 3:9, Hebrews 6:19, Ephesians 2:19-20, Philippians 1:23, I Peter 1:24-25, John 11:25-26

- John 3:5 describes salvation as a birth into a new family
- John 3:16 describes salvation as everlasting life. The word *everlasting* denotes a never-ending, never-fading condition.
- John 10:28-29 describes the protection of the Father for one of His own.
- Ephesians 1:12-14 describes the seal of the Spirit which comes when you believe. The seal indicates a finished work.
- Ephesians 2:8-9 defines salvation as a divine gift. Man cannot *earn* it by his good works,

making it impossible to *keep* it by his good
works.

⇒ **Deduction** - The Bible seems to be emphatically stating that salvation is an eternal, unlos-
able gift. What then do we do with those other
verses that seem to be stating otherwise?

Near Context of the Remote Texts

You must study the near context of each of the
problem texts, realizing that the evidence in the
Bible is against losing your salvation.

The Near Context of I Timothy 4:1 indicates
the reference has to do with prophecy concerning
the last days. It is not a reference to personal salvation. A remote contextual study on the last days
will explain this passage.

The near context of II Thessalonians 2:3 indicates a falling away from truth. It seems to be a
reference to a societal problem in the last days, not
an issue about personal salvation.

The context of II Peter gives the key that
unlocks all of the problem texts on this subject. II
Peter 2:19-22 tells a story of a sow that has been
in the father's house and returns to wallowing in
the mire. A very similar story but exactly opposite
is found in Luke 15:11-24. In this story the son
finds himself in the mire of the sow but realizes
that he is not a sow and returns to the father's
house.

⇒ **Deduction** - The passage in Hebrews 6:4-6
cannot possibly refer to losing one's salvation,
because of the number of verses that prove it is

not possible to lose one's salvation. There is a different teaching there.

Near Context

Now that we have established the fact that this passage could not be referring to the loss of one's salvation, it is imperative that we look farther to find out what it does mean.

The first thing to notice is that the chapter heading is placed right in the middle of a thought. At the end of chapter 5, the writer of Hebrews is rebuking these Christian brothers for their lack of growth. In fact, he seems to indicate that they have regressed in their walk with God.

For when for the time ye ought to be teach-ers, ye have need that one teach you again which be the first principles of the oracles of God; and are become such as have need of milk, and not of strong meat. Heb 5:12

Then he goes on to tell them that they should leave the first principles, or the "milk" of the Word, and *go on unto perfection* (Heb.6:1). Then he says that we will do this only if God permits. A similar statement is found in II Timothy 2:24-26.

It seems that the Apostle is challenging them not to fall back. He is saying that their lack of growth puts them in the danger of falling back? Falling back to what?

Historical Context

There are two things to point out here. First of all the book is addressed to "Hebrews." He is speaking to a specific ethnic group of Christians.

Yes, everyone can learn from it, but the primary group addressed are Jewish believers who had been exposed to a perverted doctrine. The mixing of law and grace.

The second historical fact to note is found in Galatians 2:11-21. Peter had fallen back to pre-grace era. Paul strongly rebuked him and Barnabas for this. Did those two men lose their salvation? Of course not! But they had presented a perverted form of the gospel, by mixing pre-Pentecost legalism with post-Pentecost grace. In Hebrews 10:26 Paul emphatically states that there is only one sacrifice for sins. Indications are that Peter and Barnabas learned from their mistake and repented (note II Peter 3:15-16). So what is the falling back mentioned? It has to refer to the Jewish people who saw the resurrection and the signs of the Holy Spirit yet chose to go back to their old Jewish ways. This caused them to enter into the blindness that was placed on them by God and therefore it became impossible for them to be saved (see Romans 11:15-25).

D. The Context Principle will define a word

One very fascinating fact about the King James Version of the English Bible is that it has a dictionary built right into the text. Words that have become archaic or obscure in their meaning are defined in the context in which they are used.

Near Context

Let's look at a few examples of these kinds of

words and how they are defined.

- In Genesis 10:18 we find the word *abroad* which has been defined as an archaic word. The dictionary says it means widespread. If you would simply look at the near context you will find that definition. The word immediately preceding *abroad* is *spread*.
- In Genesis 49:17 the translators used the word *adder*. Again the context gives an exact dictionary definition. It reads *a <u>serpent</u> by the way, an **adder*** (dictionary def. – "a serpent")
- In Genesis 17:10-11 we find the word "betwixt." You must look just a little farther than the next word. If you are reading the story here in Genesis 17, you will actually come to the definition first, so you will automatically know the meaning of the archaic word when you get to it. The definition *<u>between</u> me and you...* is found in verse 10. The archaic word is put into an identical phrase as the definition, thereby identifying it as a synonym - ***betwixt** me and you* (dictionary def. – "between").
- In Romans 7:7-14 the archaic word *concupiscence* is used. In this context we find this larger word actually defined four times for us. The dictionary defines concupiscence as: "covetousness or lust after... carnal things...unlawful." Notice the underlined words in this verse, reflecting that definition: *for I had not known <u>lust</u>, except the <u>law</u> had said, Thou shalt not <u>covet</u>. But sin, taking occasion by the commandment, wrought in me all manner of **concupiscence**.*

The Dispensation Principle

I.   The Dispensation of Innocence
II.   The Dispensation of Conscience
III. The Dispensation of Government
IV.   The Dispensation of Promise
V.   The Dispensation of Law
VI.   The Dispensation of Grace
VII. The Dispensation of the Kingdom

chapter FOUR

The Dispensation Principle

Study to shew thyself approved unto God,
a workman that needeth not to be ashamed,
rightly dividing the word of truth.
II Timothy 2:15

- Why was it considered acceptable for Abraham to marry his sister?
- Why was it okay for Jacob to have children by four different women?
- Why doesn't God appear to us like He did to Moses?
- Why don't we offer animal sacrifices to God like they did in the Old Testament?

An answer to these questions can be found in a study of what the theological world calls **THE DISPENSATIONS.** A *dispensation* is a period of time in which God deals with man in a particular way in respect to man's sin and his respon-

> ## Four Elements
> ## of a Dispensation
> 1. Man's state
> 2. Man's responsibility
> 3. Man's failure
> 4. Subsequent judgment

sibilities. God has dealt with man in seven specifically different ways. If you understand these different divisions of time, you will better understand your own responsibilities in the current dispensation of Grace.

How can you tell when a dispensation begins or ends? Did this come out of a man's imagination or is there really a dispensational framework in the Bible?

> ## *Dispensation*
>
> A period of time in which God deals with man in a particular way in respect to man's sin and his responsibilities.

As you study the Bible from an overall perspective, a pattern slowly emerges. This pattern starts with man in a particular condition. God then gives man a particular responsibility. Man then fails to uphold this responsibility because of the weakness of his flesh. Subsequent judgment follows. We then find man standing in the aftermath of that judgment. He is given another responsibility... and the cycle continues.

It is important to remember that, although God dealt with people differently in each of these dispensations, salvation has always been and always will be the same: *For by grace are ye saved through faith; and that not of yourselves: it is the gift of God: Not of works, lest any man should boast.* Ephesians 2:8-9. Hebrews 4:2 illustrates this point quite well:

> *For unto us was the gospel preached, as well as unto them: but the word preached did not profit them, not being mixed with faith in them that heard it.*

Measure each period of time by these four elements to determine the length and breadth of a dispensation.

1. Man's *state* at the beginning
2. Man's *responsibility*
3. Man's *failure*
4. Subsequent *judgment*

I. The Dispensation of Innocence
Genesis 1-3

State: began at Creation

Responsibility: to dress and keep the Garden, not to eat of the forbidden fruit; obey these simple instructions.

Failure: allowed Satan into the Garden, ate of the forbidden fruit

Judgment: curse on Man, Woman, and the serpent; expulsion from Paradise; banned from the tree of life

II. The Dispensation of Conscience
Genesis 3-8

State: began on the outside of the Garden

Responsibility: to act upon what man now knows Genesis 4:7

Failure: refused to listen to his conscience

Judgment: God sent a flood.

III. The Dispensation of Government
Genesis 8-11

State: began on the ark

Responsibility: to govern himself
Genesis 9:5-6

Failure: position of power was used for pride

Judgment: ended at Babel with God confusing the languages

IV. The Dispensation of Promise
Genesis 11– Exodus 15

State: call of God on one man (Abraham) to separate from the world he knew

Responsibility: The chosen ones were to abide in the Land of Promise.

Failure: First Abraham, then Isaac, then Jacob, and consequently generations after, found themselves constantly returning to Egypt.

Judgment: God's people became enslaved to the Egyptians.

V. The Dispensation of Law
Exodus – Gospels

State: the Exodus

Responsibility: obey the specific laws of God

Failure: They trusted in the words of man before the words of God. Matthew 15:3-9.

Judgment: worldwide dispersion of God's people, the Son of God taken from them.

VI. The Dispensation of Grace
Acts-Epistles — Revelation 18

State: the Advent of the Holy Spirit

Responsibility: to live by faith. Man was given all of history from which to learn, all of the Word of God, and the Holy Spirit.

Failure: falling away – rejection of God's Word, perversion of truth

Judgment: the Church taken out, The Great Tribulation

God gave man a variety of opportunities to try to be righteous on his own. But each dispensation merely proved the hopelessness and futility of the task.

VII. The Dispensation of the Kingdom
Revelation 19-20

State: Second Coming of the King of Kings

Responsibility: to the personal presence and reign of Jesus Christ on this earth

Failure: feigned obedience not from the heart.

Judgment: The Great White Throne

Important Notes:

1. There are five different types of government that God uses to deal with mankind throughout these seven different dispensations. See appendix C.

2. It is also interesting to see the correlation between these seven dispensations and the seven seals described in Rev. 6-19. See appendix E.

The Covenant Principle

I.   The Edenic Covenant
II.   The Adamic Covenant
III.   The Noahic Covenant
IV.   The Abrahamic Covenant
V.   The Mosaic Covenant
VI.   The Palestinian Covenant
VII.   The Davidic Covenant
VIII.   The New Covenant
IX.   The Overcomers Covenant
X.   The Tribulation Covenant
XI.   The Millenium Covenant
XII.   The Marriage Covenant

chapter *FIVE*

The Covenant Principle

For when God made promise to Abraham, because he could swear by no greater, he sware by himself, Saying, Surely blessing I will bless thee, and multiplying I will multiply thee. And so, after he had patiently endured, he obtained the promise. For men verily swear by the greater: and an oath for confirmation is to them an end of all strife. Wherein God, willing more abundantly to shew unto the heirs of promise the immutability of his counsel, confirmed it by an oath: That by two immutable things, in which it was impossible for God to lie, we might have a strong consolation, who have fled for refuge to lay hold upon the hope set before us: Which hope we have as an anchor of the soul, both sure and steadfast, and which entereth into that within the veil...
Hebrews 6:13-19

A Covenant is an agreement between God and Man. The Word of God is the explanation and demonstration of God's dealings with mankind. Dr. C.I. Scofield stated, "All Scripture crystallizes about, and is the development of, these covenants."

> *"All Scripture crystallizes about, and is the development of, these covenants."*
> **C.I. Scofield**

There are two kinds of covenants: Conditional

and Unconditional. A Conditional Covenant was based upon the faithfulness of man. An Unconditional Covenant was based upon the faithfulness of God.

Hebrews 8:6-13 mentions that there are two covenants, an old covenant and a new covenant. It is important to realize that this is a reference to the covenants made with Israel, and should not be confused with the fact that there are twelve distinct covenants made with man since the beginning of time.

Unconditional Covenants always have a sign. The most famous and noticeable of these signs is the rainbow of the Noahic Covenant. The signs God gives us are to remind us on a regular basis that He intends to keep His promises. The Conditional Covenants never have a sign.

We have divided the study of each covenant into five parts:
  A. Its kind
      (Conditional or Unconditional)
  B. The responsibilities of Man
      (What God expected him to do)
  C. The responsibilities of God
      (What God demanded of Himself)
  D. The status of the Covenant
      (Will Man's failure change the covenant,
or   can the covenant still be counted on)
  E. The proof of a covenant's dependability
      (Whether or not we can still see God's sign
      or signature)

I. Edenic Covenant
Genesis 1:28-30; 2:15-17

A. A Conditional Covenant

B. Man's Responsibilities
1. Subdue the earth
2. Replenish the earth
3. Dress the garden
4. Keep the garden
5. Not to eat of the Tree of the Knowledge of Good and Evil

C. God's Responsibilities
1. Give dominion over the animal kingdom
2. Provide a helpmeet
3. Give power to man's efforts
4. Allow man to live in the Garden of God
5. Let man live forever

D. Man failed - God is not obligated to fulfill covenant.

E. No sign given

> *The signs God gives are to remind us that He intends to keep His promises.*

II. Adamic Covenant
Genesis 3:14-19

A. An Unconditional Covenant

B. Man's Responsibilities
To continue living on the earth with the judgments of God on everything

C. God's Responsibilities
  Genesis 3:14-19   see also John 3:16-18
  1. Judgment of the serpent
  2. Judgment of the woman
  3. Judgment of the man
  4. Judgment of the entire creation
  5. Promise of a deliverer

D. God will keep His promises

E. Sign – birth

III. Noahic Covenant
  Genesis 8:20-9:17

A. An Unconditional Covenant

B. Man's Responsibilities
  1. Subdue the earth
  2. Replenish the earth
  3. Change his diet – eat meat but no blood
        See Acts 15:20
  4. Govern himself
  5. Have dominion over the animal king-
     dom - God's opinion about man and
     animal relationship didn't change.
     (note: Edenic Covenant)

C. God's Responsibilities
  1. Never again curse the earth by water
  2. Never again destroy all living
  3. Natural order of seasons established

D. Man and God are still bound by this covenant

E. Sign – Rainbow after a rain

IV. Abrahamic Covenant
Genesis 12:1-3

A. An Unconditional Covenant

B. Man's Responsibility
1. Believe God   Romans 4:3
2. Leave his homeland

C. God's Responsibility
1. *I will make of thee a great nation*
2. *I will bless thee*
3. *and make thy name great*
4. *Thou shalt be a blessing*
5. *I will give unto thee, and to thy seed ...the land of Canaan, for an everlasting possession* Genesis 17:8
6. *In thee shall all families of the earth be blessed*
7. *Thou shalt be a father of many nations* Genesis 17:4-5 Genesis 25:1-6

D. Covenant between God and Abraham's seed   Galatians 3:16

E. Sign – Circumcision

V. Mosaic Covenant
Exodus 19-20

A. An Unconditional Covenant

B. Man's Responsibilities
To obey the whole law   James 2:10
Jesus came to fulfill the law, not abolish it. Matthew 5:17

C. God's Responsibilities
1. Giving of the law
The moral law – Exodus 20
The civil law – Exodus 21-24
The ceremonial law – Exodus 25-31
2. Blessings for obedience
A Jew will be blessed now if he chooses to obey God. Obedience for a Jew in the Age of Grace requires his acceptance of the Lamb of God for his atonement.
3. Preservation of the Word of God

D. Israel failed and was subsequently punished.
Even though the Jews were punished and driven out of their land, the promises of God were left open to those who choose to turn back to God. II Chronicles 7:14

E. Sign — The Preservation of God's Word
Ex. 20:22, Ps. 138:2, Is. 40:8, Mat. 5:18, Mat. 24:35, Rom. 3:1-2

Note: *While much of the Mosaic Covenant dealt with specific actions the Jews were supposed to be engaged in, some of it is still applicable today. For example: the 10 Commandments are the basis for our laws. There was an unconditional sign given; therefore, I have to believe that this is an unconditional covenant.*

VI. Palestinian Covenant
     Deuteronomy 30:1-10

    A. An Unconditional Covenant

    B. Man's Responsibilities
       To claim the land for Jehovah

    C. God's Responsibilities
       1. The Lord will return vs. 3
       2. The people will be regathered vs. 3-5
       3. The nation will be saved vs. 6
       4. Israel will prosper and be blessed vs.9

    D. Because they failed in the Mosaic Covenant, Israel was unwillingly wrenched from the land. God is bringing them back.
        A Jew's fellowship with God is intrinsically linked to the land of promise. When she turns toward God she always begins by turning to her land. The Palestinian Covenant and the Mosaic Covenant are twin covenants in this regard.

E. Sign – The land itself

VII. Davidic Covenant
II Samuel 7:1-16

A. An Unconditional Covenant

B. Man's Responsibilities
David was given the responsibility to believe God. This covenant was given to him at the time when he wanted to build a temple for the Lord. The Lord told him by the prophet Nathan that his son would build the temple.

C. God's Responsibilities
God promised to build a house for David that would last forever. He also promised to establish an eternal throne under David's name and a Kingdom.

D. Fulfilled in Christ
- This covenant is a beautiful prophecy of the coming Kingdom of the Son of God. Notice that it is the Son of the King that builds the temple.
- The only One that can claim clear title to the throne is Jesus. He has right to the throne because He is the legal firstborn son of Joseph (Matthew 1:1-17). Because He is adopted by Joseph and not his actual son, Jesus misses

the curse that was placed on the line of Jechoniah (see the curse of Coniah, Jeremiah 22:24-30).

E. Sign – The Son   Isaiah 7:14

Isaiah's prophecy contains a double reference. The Hebrew word chosen to represent the virgin is the word álmah (almaŵ). This word is unique in that it can mean virgin or young woman. The prophecy of Immanuel is clearly pointing to Christ and His virgin birth (Matthew 1:23). Yet it is also pointing to an event in Isaiah's immediate future (Isaiah 8:3) in which Isaiah's wife was to give birth to a son. The son of Isaiah was a sign to Israel that a ruler would be born for them.

VIII. New Covenant

Jeremiah 31:31-34, Hebrews 8:6-13
Hebrews 13:20

A. An Unconditional Covenant

It is important to note that this is an unconditional covenant with those to whom it is given. It is a free gift and cannot be earned. Romans Chapter 9 teaches us that God chooses who will fall under this covenant. Romans Chapter 10 shows us the wonderful truth that God's choice is whosover will call upon the name of the Lord.

B. Man's Responsibilities

In this new covenant man is given the responsibility to accept the gift of grace through faith (Ephesians 2:8-9). He is to be "born again" (John 3) into the family of God by a miracle which God alone can perform, but which he can have by exercising his free will and asking for it (Romans 10:13).

C. God's Responsibilities

Under the Old Covenant, God wrote His Law in stone. Under the New Covenant, God wrote the Law in "fleshy tables of the heart" (II Corinthians 3:3). In this New Covenant, God takes upon Himself the responsibility to forgive us, sanctify us, and give us all things that pertain to life and godliness through the knowledge of Jesus Christ (II Peter 1:3).

D. This Covenant will carry us into the Kingdom.

E. Sign – The seal of the Spirit   Eph. 1:13; 4:30, 2 Cor. 1:22, Rom. 8:16, Heb. 10:15

Note: *It has been asserted that the sign of the New Covenant was the cloven tongues of fire. This, however, is inaccurate because the cloven tongues of fire are not still visible today. A more accurate interpretation then would be that the sign of the New*

Covenant is the seal of the Holy Spirit which is eternally ours, and definitely a continual witness within us.

IX. Overcomer's Covenant
Revelation 2-3

A. An Unconditional Covenant
This is an unconditional covenant in the same sense that the New Covenant is unconditional. Those who receive these promises have chosen to follow God.

B. Man's Responsibilities
To overcome with the power of God. There is only one way to overcome, that is by faith. Ephesians 2:8-9, I John 5:4-5

C. God's Responsibilities
1. Restore access to the Tree of Life
   Revelation 2:7
2. Provide escape from the judgment of the Adamic Covenant
   Revelation 2:11
3. Give him a new name
   Revelation 2:17; 3:12
4. Grant him power over the nations
   Revelation 2:26
5. Preserve his name in the book of life
   Revelation 3:5
6. Give him New Jerusalem (Promised land)
   Revelation 3:12

7. Give him a throne
Revelation 3:21

D. These are promises that will last forever.

E. Sign: There was a sign given for each of these seven promises. The sign is given in each of the first seven covenants. Everything that was not completely *fulfilled* in the first seven covenants is *filled full* in this covenant.

X. Tribulation Covenant
Rev. 14:9-13

A. An Unconditional Covenant

B. Man's Responsibilities
To make a choice between taking the mark of the beast or not taking it.

C. God's Responsibilities
Those who do not take the mark will be blessed. See Rev. 13:15, 14:13, 15:2, 20:4

D. This covenant is like the last two in that man is given the opportunity to make a choice. The benefits are directly linked to his choice. The covenant will last for the duration of the kingdom of the beast.
E. Sign: The mark of the beast

XI. Millennium Covenant
Rev. 19:5-8 Rev. 20:1-4

A. A Conditional Covenant
This is a conditional covenant in the same sense as the Edenic Covenant. It is made not with the Bride of Christ, who is now in her glorified state, but with the nations that were not turned into hell (Psalm 9:17) at the end of the Tribulation.

B. Man's Responsibilities -
To praise God and obey His servants

C. God's Responsibilities
1. Bind Satan for 1,000 years
2. Rule in person
3. Prepare His Bride
4. Cleanse the world Rev. 20:11-15

D. This is a fulfillment of the Davidic Covenant.
It is also the Pre-Wedding preparation. Rev. 21:1-2

E. No sign given

XII. Marriage Covenant
Rev. 21:3-8

A. An Unconditional Covenant

B. Man's Responsibilities
Enjoy the presence of God

C. God's Responsibilities
   a. Wipe away the tears
   b. End of death
   c. End of sorrow
   d. End of crying
   e. End of pain
   f. End of former things
   g. Give us the inheritance of all things

D. This is the real New World Order. This is the marriage of Christ and the Church

E. Sign – God himself shall be with them and be their God

Important notes:

1. Many claim the Tribulation will be the purification of the Church. I believe this is incorrect. The preparation of the bride is to put on wedding garments, not to be tormented by the bridegroom! Look at Ephesians 5:25-28, Rev. 19:7-8, Rev. 21:1-2, 9.

2. The actual marriage takes place between Revelation 21:2 and Revelation 21:9. Note that verse two says she is "prepared as a bride" and verse nine says "the bride, the Lamb's wife." Between those verses these things take place:

   verse 3 – the Bridegroom joins the bride

> *verse 4* – the former things are forgotten by the bride ("forgetting all others")
> *verse 5* – a new beginning
> *verse 5* – the marriage certificate
> *verse 6* – the name established
> *verses 6&7* – the vows
>> *vs. 6* - His provisions given freely
>> *vs. 7* - His things given freely
> *verse 8* – "turning from all others shall cleave only to His wife"

- *For an interesting look at the Jewish Wedding ceremony see Appendix D.*

3. It is possible that the Tribulation is actually a response to the prayers of the saints.
   - The golden vials are the prayers   Rev. 5:8
   - The prayers for vengeance Rev. 6:9-10
   - The prayers mixed with incense Rev. 8:3-5
   - The vials filled with the wrath of God Rev.16:1
   - Compare to Psalm 18:6-19

The Ethnic Principle

I. The Called-out People—The Gentiles
    A. The Fathers of all the Earth
    B. The Prophecies about the Gentiles
    C. The Dividing of the Nations

II. The Called-out Race—The Israelites
    A. Abram was called
    B. Jacob developed
    C. Egypt was the growing ground
    D. The Law given
    E. The Rule of the Judges
    F. The Rule of the Kings
    G. The Throne of David established
    H. The Messiah
    I. The Scriptures

III. The Called-out Kingdom—The Church
    A. The Middle Wall broken
    B. Equality Established
    C. Israel accepts the Gentiles

chapter SIX

The Ethnic Principle

*Wherefore remember, that ye being in time past Gentiles
in the flesh, who are called Uncircumcision by that which
is called the Circumcision in the flesh made by hands;
That at that time ye were without Christ, being aliens from
the commonwealth of Israel, and strangers from the covenants of promise, having no hope, and without God in the
world: But now in Christ Jesus ye who sometimes were far
off are made nigh by the blood of Christ.*
Ephesians 2:11-13

There are three distinct ethnic divisions in the
Bible: the Jew, the Gentile, and the Church of
God. The Lord addresses each one of these ethnic
groups differently. There are promises for the Jews
that do not apply to the Gentile or the Church.
Likewise, there are promises to the Church that do
not apply to the Jew or the Gentile.

*Give none offence, neither to the Jews, nor
to the Gentiles, nor to the church of God...*
I Corinthians 10:32

Adam		Noah		Shem	
Was contemporary with		*Was contemporary with*		*Was contemporary with*	
	Years		Years		Years
Lamech	56	Lamech	595	Lamech	93
Methuselah	243	Methuselah	600	Methuselah	98
Jared	470	Jared	366	Noah	448
Mahalaleel	535	Mahalaleel	234	*After the flood*	
Cainan	605	Cainan	179	Abraham	150
Enos	695	Enos	84	Isaac	50

I. The Called-out People – Gentiles

Genesis 6:5-14

The first group of people to be called out of the world are the descendants of Noah. These are properly called Gentiles. The Hebrew word **gowy** is the base word that is translated *Gentiles*. It is first used in Genesis 10:5 and means simply a massing of bodies or people. It later came to be a term of derision used by the Jews to describe the heathen, but this was not its first use. Noah's descendants were actually God's people separated out from the condemned world. To see the overlapping lives of the Patriarchs, see the chart above.

A. The Fathers of all the Earth

Ham, Shem, Japheth Genesis 5:32

These three are called the "Fathers of all the Earth" (Genesis 9:18-19), because all nations come from them. The differences in the races actually come more from a twist in chromosomes that continued from generation to generation than they do from the different climates, as the evolutionary theories suggest. The different groups migrated to the areas they were most comfortable in (Gen. 11:1-9).

A scientific study will find that some Hamites are black and some are not. Some Shemites are Chinese, some are Israeli. The children of Japheth also have a wide variety of features and skin colors that are not exclusive to their race.

B. The Prophecies about Shem, Japheth, and Ham
> Gen. 9:25-27

Shem –
- Blessed be the Lord God of Shem
- Canaan will be the servant of Shem
- Japheth will live in the tents of Shem

Japheth – **the elder** (Genesis 10:21)
- God shall enlarge Japheth
- He will live in the tents of Shem
- Canaan will be his servant

Ham – **the younger** (Genesis 9:24)
- There is a striking absence of a blessing on Ham, although he himself was not cursed, nor were all of his descendants.
- It was the son of Ham who received the curse

Note: *The descendants of Canaan are listed in Gen. 10:15-19, Leviticus 18:3, 24-29. Only Canaan was judged - not all of the descendants of Ham. Israel was to carry out this judgment on Canaan. Rember that the land of Canaan was promised to them.*

C. The Dividing of the Nations
> Genesis 11:1-9

At the Tower of Babel all of the Hamites, Shemites and Japhethites began working together to build a tower to heaven. God decided to stop their efforts by changing their languages

What happened at the tower of Babel? Did God separate the races? Let's look at what the Bible actually says about this. First you must notice that the division mentioned is a communication division—a division of the languages. There is no mention of a division of races at this point. Later in the New Testament (Acts 17:26), the apostle clearly states that we are all of one blood.

Note:

It is interesting to note that God did not seem to be upset when the descendants of Noah's three sons crossed family lines. Note Gen. 12:1-15, Song of Solomon 1:1-6. When it comes to this issue a truthful Bible student must not let prejudice cloud his Bible study.

As to the question of inter-racial marriage, I must give my judgment at this point. Some have made a doctrine out of the separation of skin colors. As we find in the story of Moses and his wife, God does not seem to make an issue about it. In fact when the sister of Moses began to make an issue about his black wife, she was the one who received the judgment from God. There is absolutely no scripture that will support prejudice.

Racial prejudice has been a problem since Old Testament times. The only clear scriptural distinction between the races is the Gentiles and Israel (See 2. The Called-out Race). Even then God

*did not have the same view as Israel did. The story
of Jonah is an illustration of that. And then finally
Paul tells us in Ephesians that even that racial division is no more. "For he is our peace, who hath
made both one, and hath broken down the middle
wall of partition between us." Ephesians 2:14 (See
3. The Called-out Kingdom).*

II. The Called-out Race – Israel

    A. Abram was called out of the rubble of the tower of Babel. Genesis 12:1-3

Peleg lived 18 more years after Abram was born. This is interesting to note because it was in the days of Peleg that the earth was divided. It is very possible that Abram was alive when the tower of Babel was being built.

    B. The nation developed under Jacob.

His 12 sons were the heads of the 12 tribes. See Genesis 49:1-33

Reuben, Simeon, Levi, Judah, Zebulun, Issachar, Dan, Gad, Asher, Naphtali, Benjamin.

No tribe was named for Joseph, but his sons, Ephraim and Manasseh, each lay claim to a half portion of the tribe.

    C. Egypt was the growing ground.

    D. Sinai was where the Law was given.

    E. Through the book of Judges Israel was ruled tribe by tribe.

    F. Finally they got a king after their own heart – Saul.

G. Then the Throne of David was given to Israel.

H. Messiah came through Israel – Jesus Christ.

I. The Scriptures were committed to Israel Romans 3:2

III. The Called-out Kingdom – the Church
I Peter 2:9-12

A. The middle wall of partition is broken down between the called-out people and the called-out race.
Ephesians 2:11-22

B. In the new kingdom there is no difference between the Jew and the Greek. The word Greek was used here as a synonym for Gentile because of the political climate in which Paul lived.
Romans 10:12

C. Even the Jewish believers, after much heated debate, had to conclude that the Gentiles were to be included in this new kingdom.
Acts 15:13-35

Note:

There is some debate as to whether there is a "Universal Church." I've noticed, however, that no matter how heated the rhetoric gets and no matter how you define it, every Bible student must come to the conclusion that there is or will be a gathering together of all believers at some point.

The word church (εκλεσια) literally means

"called out." Depending on the context in which it is used, it might have the emphasis of an assembly (called out to); this is how it is used in Acts 19:32,39,and 41. However, it can also, have the implication of a harvest (called out from) as we find in Acts 7:38. This is the sense in which we are using it here. It is more of a national identification than a specific gathering or assembly.

It would be beneficial to the Bible student to look up every Bible reference which uses this word (most often translated "church") and make a chart identifying the meaning of the word by each context in which it is used. This will be much more profitable than getting into a debate regarding whether or not there is a Universal Church. These verses, with the author's understanding, are listed in Appendix B.

The Agreement Principle

I. A Look at God's Promises
       A. The Faithfulness of God
       B. The Truthfulness of God's Word
       C. The Responsibility of the Student

II. A Look at some Discrepancies
       A. Conflicts in spelling
       B. Different people with the same names
       C. One person with different names
       D. Different places with the same name
       E. Different names for the same place

chapter *SEVEN*

The Agreement Principle

*Wherein God, willing more abundantly to shew
unto the heirs of promise the immutability of his
counsel, confirmed it by an oath: That by two immutable things, in which it was impossible for God to
lie, we might have a strong consolation, who have
fled for refuge to lay hold upon the hope set before
us: Which hope we have as an anchor of the soul,
both sure and stedfast, and which entereth into that
within the veil... Hebrews 6:17-19*

This principle states that the Truthfulness and
Faithfulness of God guarantee that the Bible will
not contradict itself. Starting from this point we
can look at the seeming contradictions of the Bible
without fear, knowing that there are answers to the
difficulties, because God cannot lie.

In this chapter we will first look at what the
Scripture says about God's Faithfulness and Truthfulness, and then we will try to examine briefly a
few of the apparent contradictions. This will not be
an exhaustive study of such contradictions. It is
merely a reminder to always be confident in the
unity of the Bible. It is a tool to keep handy when
you run up against confusion.

I. A Look at God's Promises

A. The Faithfulness of God
- "To all generations"
    Psalm 119:90
- "Reacheth to the clouds"
    Psalm 36:5
- The covenant He will not break
    Psalm 89:34-35
- "Great is thy faithfulness"
    Lamentations 3:23
- God cannot lie
    Hebrews 6:16-19 Titus 1:2
- "His work is perfect"
    Deuteronomy 32:4

B. The Trustworthiness of God's Word
- "Thy word is truth"
    John 17:17
- All Scripture is given by God
    II Timothy 3:16
- "Settled in heaven"
    Psalm 119:89
- "True from the beginning"
    Psalm 119:160
- Magnified above His name
    Psalm 138:2

C. The Responsibility of the Student
- Rightly divide the Word of Truth
        II Timothy 2:15

II. Identifying some apparent difficulties

Now that we have established that the Bible cannot contradict itself because God agrees with Himself, let's take a brief look at the reasons for some apparent contradictions.

A. Conflicts in spelling

Rahab (OT) = Rachab (NT) Matthew 1:5
Boaz (OT) = Booz (NT) Matthew 1:5
Joshua (OT) = Jesus (NT) Acts 7:45

This problem comes because of the fact the Old Testament was penned in Hebrew for the most part, and the New Testament was penned in Greek. When the translators came to proper names, rather than actually translate them, they did something called "transliteration." Transliteration is the process of giving each letter in the original language an English equivalent. The New Testament names are either translated or transliterated from the Hebrew to the Greek before being transliterated to the English.

> *All apparent discrepancies can be explained because God cannot lie!*

B. Different people with the same name

Common sense will reveal that there are different people with the same name in the

Scripture. Some names in Bible times were more popular than others, just like in our times. We have listed here a few examples:

10 Simons - Simon; Simon Peter; Simon Zelotes; Simon, the son of Joseph and Mary; Simon, the father of Judas Iscariot; Simon, the Pharisee; Simon, the leper; Simon, the Cyrenian; Simon, the tanner; and Simon Magus

3 James – James, the son of Zebedee; James, the son of Alphaeus; James, the Lord's brother

6 Herods – Herod the Great; Herod Antipas; Herod Archelaus; Herod Philip; Herod Agrippa I; Herod Agrippa II

6 Marys – Mary, the mother of Jesus; Mary, the mother of James; Mary, the mother of John; Mary Magdelene; Mary of Bethany; Mary, a helper of Paul

C. One person with different names

Sometimes you will find that one person has more than one name to which he would answer. He might be referred to by a surname, as in Mark 3:16 were Jesus gave Simon the name Peter.   In Acts 1:23 we find a man named Joseph who was called Barsabas, which was evidently a nickname, and then was surnamed Justus. The following list demonstrates some of the different names that can be found.

Silvanus was also called Silas
Levi was also called Matthew
Timotheus was also called Timothy
Cephas was also called Peter
Jehoiachin was called Jeconiah and Coniah
Saul was changed to Paul
Abram was changed to Abraham
Sarai was changed to Sarah
Jacob was changed to Israel
Joseph was changed to Zaphnath-paaneah
Daniel was changed to Belteshazzar
Hananiah was changed to Shadrach
Mishael was changed to Meshach
Azariah was changed to Abednego

D. Different places with the same name

There can be some confusion when the Bible student doesn't realize that two different towns may have the same name. For example: there are three different Bethsaidas, and five different Romas.

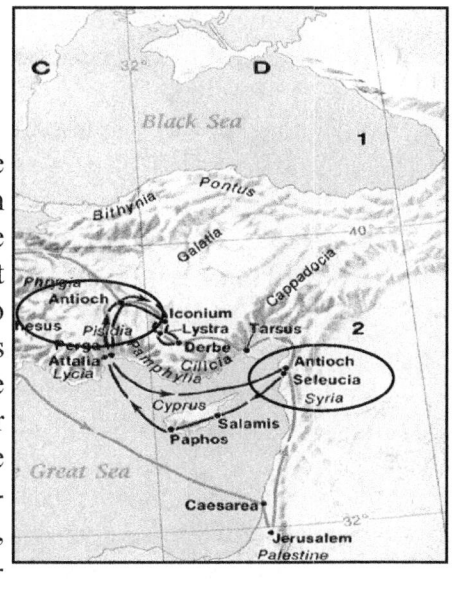

Acts 13:1 tells us that Paul and Barnabas were

teachers in the church at Antioch when the Lord called them to do missionary work. Acts 13:4 tells us that in their missionary journeys they arrived in Antioch and began to preach in the synagogue. On the map of Pauls missionary journeys on page 83 notice the two different Antiochs. There was an Antioch of Syria were Paul and Barnabas had been teachers, and then there was an Antioch of Pisidia which they found on their missionary journey.

E. Different names but the same place

As it is with people, so it is with places—sometimes there are different names for the same place. The Sea of Galilee was also called Lake Gennesaret (Luke 5:1). This name probably came from the country that it was in, the land of Gennesaret (Mark 14:34). Other folks called it the Sea of Tiberias (John 6:1), and still others called it Chinnereth (Joshua 13:27). I suppose where you were from had a lot to do with what you called it.

The Dead Sea also had several names. In Ezekiel 47:18 it is called the East Sea. In Deuteronomy 3:17 it is called both the Sea of the Plain and the Salt Sea.

• There are many places in the Bible that have been termed discrepancies by "scholars" which can be explained as simply as we have done here. Some of the difficulties are more difficult to unravel. Whenever the Bible student comes upon one

of these apparent differences he should first remember the promises laid out at the beginning of
this chapter, and then, armed with diligence and
faith, search for the answer.

The Direct Statement Principle

I.   Words mean What Words Mean
     A. The Curse of Canaan
     B. The Resurrection of Christ

II. When common sense makes sense, make no
     other sense
     A. The Tongues of Angels
     B. The New Jerusalem is not Heaven

III. Figures of speech are not literal statements
     A. The Metaphor
     B. The Simile
     C. The Metonymy
     D. The Hyperbole

chapter EIGHT

The Direct Statement Principle

God is not a man, that he should lie; neither the
son of man, that he should repent: hath he said,
and shall he not do it? or hath he spoken, and
shall he not make it good? Numbers 23:19

It is important for the Bible student to understand that God says what He means and means what He says. The Direct Statement Principle teaches and supports that fact.

I. "Words mean what words mean."

The first understanding of any Bible passage should come from the obvious meaning of the text. Take the words for exactly what they say instead of what you have heard they said, or what you think they said.

A. The curse of Canaan Genesis 9:19-27

An example of how important this principle is can be found in the discussion of the curse of Canaan. Some have misread the Bible text assuming that Ham and his lineage were cursed, when this is not the case. Let's take a quick look at what the Bible specifically says.

> *"Words mean what words mean"*
> D.R. Haifley

This story is an incomplete one. It is unclear what Ham did that was wrong (vs. 24). Some speculate that he had committed some kind of sodomite act against his father. I personally don't believe this to be the case. Due to the status of a father in that culture the disrespect Ham showed was appalling and caused the curse upon his lineage. What he actually did is stated in verse 22.

- He told his brothers that his father was uncovered, instead of dealing with it himself.
- They did the right thing to hide his shame.
- The action of Shem and Japheth made Noah aware of the situation.

The question that follows then is "Who was cursed?" The Bible says it was Canaan, who was only one of the four sons of Ham. These are listed in Genesis 10:6-10. The Canaanites (the children of Canaan) are listed in verses 15-18, and the geographical boundaries in which they settled are specified in verse 19. It is obvious that one of the commissions of the Israelites was to fulfill the curse of God on Canaan by utterly destroying them and then by possessing their land.

B. The Resurrection of Christ

Another example of the importance of this principle can be found in the discussion surrounding the resurrection of Christ. For many years self-styled theologians have debated whether there was a literal resurrection. It has been said that possibly the resurrection was a spiritual one, and that the disciples of Christ merely sensed his resurrection and did not actually see it. Some have gone so far as to say that Jesus did not actually die on the cross - He just passed out and was revived by the coolness of the tomb. Their questions and doubts are quickly laid to rest by applying the Direct Statement Principle.

The Bible clearly states that the disciples in Luke 24 actually saw Jesus, they talked with Him, and they ate with Him. In I Corinthians 15:1-8 the Apostle Paul testifies that over 500 brethren had seen Jesus after His resurrection at one time, and most of them were still alive at the time of the writing of I Corinthians. He also gave specific names of trustworthy people who were living at that time and could verify the story.

In I Corinthians 15:12-23, Paul makes the accurate case that, if Jesus had not literally raised from the dead, than we as Christians are wasting our miserable lives for nothing. The martyrs have died for nothing. The preachers are preaching for nothing. And we are yet dead in our sins with no hope of ever communicating with our Maker.

Without doubt, Jesus raised from the dead literally three days after his death.

II. "When common sense makes sense, make no other sense."

As you have been studying hermeneutics, you've probably noticed that most of the principles set forth in this book are common sense ideas. As we stated in the preface, many generations of scholars have found these tools to be helpful in their study, but the tools have been discovered by applying common sense principles. The application of the Direct Statement Principle is one of the clearest examples of this truth.

In the next few paragraphs you will see two examples of how applying simple common sense in a direct statement will unravel generations of confusion.

A. <u>The Tongues of Angels</u>

The gift of tongues is an interesting gift. It is one that causes much confusion in those who do not take the time to study what the Bible says about it. The way to understand something like this is to start with what you know to be true and then let the Lord build on that through His Word.

Words are powerful. They were first used to build the universe (Psalms 33:6-9). Then we find that God gave them as a gift to the world. Eve did not think it strange to be conversing with a serpent (Genesis 3:1-5). Could it be that this was a common occurrence for even the animals to speak in the Garden of Eden? After the fall there is no indication that animals were able to speak again, except in the case of Balaam's ass. Communication then became the sole prize and possession of those who were made in the image of God, humans.

The Bible teaches us in Genesis 11:1 that the whole earth had one language or, you might say, "one tongue." Everyone was able to understand everyone else. However, because the people decided to build a tower to heaven, which was a violation of God's will, God chose to divide the languages. In the Bible this group of languages is called "The tongues of men." In Acts 2:8-11 the first manifestation of the "gift of tongues" was simply the wonderful Gospel of Christ in the mother tongue of everyone listening. I believe this fact is without dispute.

The debate comes when we find a difference between the tongues of men and the tongues of angels (I Corinthians 13:1). What are these tongues of angels? Here is where the Direct Statement Principle comes in handy.

> *"When common sense makes sense - make no other sense."*
> M.G. Cambron

Let's go back and find out what kind of communication, or speech, or language, or tongue angels historically used. There are over 800 verses in the Bible that speak of angels or that record things that angels said. Isaiah 6:6-7, Daniel 9:20-22 and Matthew 1:20 are just a few examples. In each case you will find the person being spoken too understands the angel (a little common sense needed here). Did the angels have to take a crash course in that language, or is there a tongue of angels that anyone listening will understand?

Using exactly what the Bible says (Direct Statement) about the tongues of men and of angels —nothing more, nothing less—it appears that the tongues of angels were used in Acts 2:8-11.

But that doesn't explain it all, does it? You must continue in this same way to understand all that the Bible says about tongues. Take each element and define it using every reference in the Bible that you can find on the subject and applying common sense.

B. <u>The New Jerusalem is not Heaven</u>

The next demonstration of the importance of the Direct Statement principle can be found in the misunderstanding of the New Jerusalem and Heaven.

Most of us have heard of the streets of gold that are in Heaven were God lives. Yet the truth is that we find hardly any reference to God's abode, and we also find very few glimpses of it. The streets of gold (Revelation 21:21) are actually in the New Jerusalem which comes down out of Heaven (Revelation 21:1-2). In Revelation 21-22 we find that God actually has to make a New Heaven and a New Earth so that he can live with us. It's interesting to note that God's Home cannot accommodate us and our home cannot accommodate Him in His Glorified Form. Therefore He must make a new place for us to be able to come together and live.

III. Figures of Speech

A figure of speech is a beautiful tool that the Lord uses many times in the Scripture to express a literal truth in a colorful way. It should not be taken literally, but figuratively in the sense in which it is spoken. We commonly use this method of communication in our language. You've probably heard or used these phrases: "His bread isn't quite done," "Stabbed in the back," "He can't see what I'm talking about," "Let sleeping dogs lie." Imagine someone trying to translate those statements literally into another language. They don't actually mean what the say literally but are instead a figure of the truth. (Note Hebrews 9:9; Hebrews 11:19, I Peter 3:21 to see how God uses a figure to communicate the truth.)

When should we take a passage of Scripture literally, or figuratively? Words should be understood in their literal sense unless such literal interpretation involves a manifest contradiction or absurdity.

The following examples are obviously not literal statements:

- *For, behold, I have made thee this day a defenced city, and an iron pillar, and brasen walls against the whole land, against the kings of Judah, against the princes thereof, against the priests thereof, and against the people of the land.* Jeremiah 1:18

  Jeremiah was not a literal defenced city,

nor was he made into an iron pillar, nor brazen walls. These were pictures of how God was going to use him in a spiritual way.

- *But Jesus said unto him, Follow me; and let the dead bury their dead.*
                              Matthew 8:22

Jesus was not teaching that you should leave your dead loved ones lying in the street for those who had already died to take care of. This is not even possible nor is it respectful. He was using a figure of speech to point out to this man that he had a spiritual calling.

- *And if thy right eye offend thee, pluck it out, and cast it from thee: for it is profitable for thee that one of thy members should perish, and not that thy whole body should be cast into hell.* Matthew 5:29

The Lord is not literally telling you to disfigure your body. There are other scriptures that indicate this could not be true (ie., Leviticus 19:28). Again He is using a figure of speech to show the importance of a spiritual concept.

There are over 200 kinds of figures of speech in the English language. Common sense is needed to interpret them. Here we have listed four of the most commonly used figures of speech.

A. THE METAPHOR: *Stating one thing and meaning another.* Notice in these phases that one person or thing is said to be something else. It is actually a comparative description.

> Galatians 2:9 *who seemed to be pillars*
> Psalm 18:2 *The Lord is my rock*
> Isaiah 40:6 *flesh is grass*
> I Corinthians 11:23-24 *bread is my body*

B. THE SIMILE: *Likening one thing to another.* The key word in a simile is "as"

> Revelation 21:2 the New Jerusalem *as* a
> bride
> Genesis 3:22 man *as* one of Us
> I Samuel 15:23 rebellion *as* witchcraft

C. THE METONYMY: *One noun is substituted for another that is not a pronoun.*

> John 4:10-14 The reference to living water speaks of salvation
> Obadiah 8-10 Esau and Jacob actually refers to entire nations

D. THE HYPERBOLE: *An exaggeration or magnification beyond reality.*

> John 21:25 *the world itself could not contain the books*
> Job 3:3 *Let the day perish wherein I was born*

First Mention Principle

I. Identifying the work and style of Key Players
    A. God the Father
    B. God the Holy Spirit
    C. God the Son
    D. Satan
II. Identifying a Prophetical Reference
    A. Fig Leaves
    B. Her Seed
    C. Babylon
III. Identifying a Spiritual Truth
    A. Walking in the Spirit
    B. Righteousness

chapter NINE

The First Mention Principle

For I am the LORD, I change not...
Malachi 3:6

The first time a thing is mentioned in the Word of God you will find the truth that will carry it all the way through the Scriptures.

Benjamin Wills Newton said, *I have found in the Scriptures a principle of interpretation which I believe, if conscientiously adopted, will serve as an unfailing guide to the Mind of God as contained there. The first mentioned thing (the very first words of any subject of which the Holy Spirit is going to speak) is the keystone of the whole matter.*

> *"This is the law we have long since noticed and have never yet found to fail."*
> M.R. DeHaan

Dr. M.R. DeHaan said, *This is the law we have long since noticed and have never yet found to fail. The first occurrence of a word, or an expression, or an utterance is the key to subsequent meanings, or at least a guide to the essential point connected with it.*

Since there is only one speaker (Hebrews 11:1) throughout the Bible, He can shape what is being said so that it directly links with that which follows.

Simply put – This principle introduces a person, place or thing that maintains its character throughout the entire Bible. You can see this principle in other books, where the author will introduce the main characters and possibly even the direction of the story in the first few chapters. Newspaper articles are also designed this way so that you can get a preview of the entire article in just a few lines.

I. Identifying the work and style of Key Players in Scripture

A. God—

Genesis 1:1 says, *In the beginning God created.* God is identified here as the source of all things. All things that we know and understand begin with Him.

Proverbs 1:7 reaffirms this concept when it says, *The fear of the Lord is the beginning of knowledge.*

Revelation 22:13 once again states this truth, *I am Alpha and Omega, the beginning and the end, the first and the last.*

B. The Holy Spirit–

Genesis 1:2 explains the work of the Holy

Spirit and His redemptive mission. *....And the earth was without form, and void; and darkness was upon the face of the deep. And the Spirit of God moved upon the face of the waters.* This verse reveals the presence of the Holy Spirit in the work of God and identifies His role in it.

Jesus explains in John 4:24, "God is a Spirit: and they that worship him must worship him in spirit and in truth."

Once again we find Him in the end of the Book, Revelation 22:17, *And the Spirit and the bride say, Come...*

C. Jesus Christ–

Genesis 1:3 gives us the first glimpse of the Son of God: *And God said, Let their be light: and there was light.* Notice the difference between this statement and all the other statements of Creation. In each act of creation we see the word, *made.* But in this act of creation the Bible says there *was* light. Light already existed.

John 1:7-9 reveals that the Light was Jesus Christ. *The same came for a witness, to bear witness of the Light, that all men through him might believe. He was not that Light, but was sent to bear witness of that Light. That was the true Light, which lighteth every man that cometh into the world.* John chapter 1 has more to say that clearly identifies Jesus with that Light. If you trace the path of light through the Scriptures, you will learn more about the character of Jesus. For example: think about the rainbow, which is the promise of God. It is broken light.

Revelation 21:23 confirms the presence of

Christ the Light, *And the city had no need of the sun, neither of the moon, to shine in it: for the glory of God did lighten it, and Lamb is the light thereof.*

D. Satan–

Genesis 3:1 gives us our first look at Satan. Here we see his subtlety and his motives: *...Yea, hath God said...?* From the very beginning his primary objective has been to cast doubt on the Word of God.

II Corinthians 11:3 reminds us of his desire to corrupt us. *But I fear, lest by any means, as the serpent beguiled Eve through his subtilty, so your minds should be corrupted from the simplicity that is in Christ.* This knowledge gives us some understanding into the Lord's reference to vipers in Matthew 23:33-34 and John 8:44. He was not being nasty to the Pharisees. His name-calling was merely an identification with the original viper. It was meant to be a revelation to the hearers that the whole emphasis of the Pharisees was to corrupt the Word of God.

II Corinthians 2:11 states that we know what Satan's devices are. *Lest Satan should get an advantage of us: for we are not ignorant of his devices.*

Revelation 20:10 gives us our final look at Satan. *And the devil that deceived them was cast into the lake of fire and brimstone, where the beast and the false prophet are, and shall be tormented day and night for ever and ever.* This is the complete and utter victory over the deceiver. Hallelujah!

E. Others–

There is not time or space here to continue to identify the key players of Scripture. However, you will find it interesting to follow this same line of study for Adam, Eve, Cain, Abel, Seth. There is much that can be learned about man, man's sin, and the answer to man's condemnation, by studying these characters.

II. Identifying a Prophetical Reference

A. Fig Leaves–

Matthew 24:32-33 gives us a mile marker or sign for the Lord's return. Matt 24:32-34, *Now learn a parable of the fig tree; When his branch is yet tender, and putteth forth leaves, ye know that summer is nigh: So likewise ye, when ye shall see all these things, know that it is near, even at the doors. Verily I say unto you, This generation shall not pass, till all these things be fulfilled.* This is supposed to tell us something about His return. But what?

Tracing through the Bible, we find over 40 references to fig trees. In Song of Solomon 2:13 we find this reference which appears to be what the Lord was referring to in His parable: *The fig tree putteth forth her green figs, and the vines with the tender grape give a good smell. Arise, my love, my fair one, and come away.* There is an obvious reference here to the rapture of the church, the bride, at the time of new figs.

> "The first mentioned thing is the keystone of the whole matter."
>
> B.W. Newton

What we are looking for is the first mention of the fig leaves to give us an idea of what Jesus was talking about. In Genesis 3:7 we find it: *And the eyes of them both were opened, and they knew that they were naked; and they sewed fig leaves together, and made themselves aprons.* Here is the clue we are looking for.

Fig leaves were first used to cover the results of sin in Adam and Eve. In Matthew 24 they refer to Israel's covering of the results of her sin. That is, her efforts to establish a Nation without a deliverer. This is the sign we should look for — Israel trying to establish her own righteousness without a Messiah.

B. Her Seed–

In Revelation 12:17 the Apostle John gives a description of the last half of the Tribulation Period.

> *And the dragon was wroth with the woman, and went to make war with the remnant of her seed, which keep the commandments of God, and have the testimony of Jesus Christ.*

Who is the "remnant of her seed"? Who is the dragon fighting with? You must apply the first mention principle to find out.

The first time that "her seed" is mentioned is in Genesis 3:15. It is found in the curse that was placed upon the serpent after he had deceived Eve.

> *And I will put enmity between thee and the woman, and between thy seed and her seed; it shall bruise thy head, and thou*

shalt bruise his heel.

It is the first prophecy of the coming Messiah, the Saviour of mankind. It is an obvious first reference to the virgin birth, and it also gives a pre-Roman era look at the crucifixion.

Using this first mention of the subject as a guide, we deduct that "her seed" is Jesus Christ.

> *But when the fulness of the time was come, God sent forth his Son, <u>made of a woman,</u> made under the law, To redeem them that were under the law, that we might receive the adoption of sons. And because ye are sons, God hath sent forth the Spirit of his Son into your hearts, crying, Abba, Father.*
>
> Galatians 4:4-6

The *remnant of her seed, which keep the commandments of God, and have the testimony of Jesus Christ* must be a reference to those who have placed their faith in the One who is "her seed." They must be Christians. This would confirm that there will be Christians in the Tribulation. However, remember that this is the last half of the Great Tribulation.

I must make mention here of the new theology called the "Pre-Wrath Rapture" which is a remake of other theologies that have come at us in different ages (Note II Timothy 2:18). While I believe that the perpetrators of this "new" doctrine are sincere Bible students. I believe that their hermeneutical process is faulty. There is not room here to deal with this subject in its entirety. Perhaps another book should address this subject. Let me just say that although I find Christians in the

Tribulation these are not part of the "first resurrection" mentioned in Rev. 20:5-6 and in I Thess.
4:13-18.

C. Babylon (Babel)—
There have been many questions about the
city of Babylon mentioned in Revelation 18. Is this
an actual city? Is it a country? Is it talking about
the United Nations? As we have already presented,
if you want to understand a prophetic reference, go
to its first mention in the Bible and you will begin
to understand its significance.

Genesis 10:8-10 is the first time Babel is
used. This passage gives us a peek at who founded
the city and what his condition was before the
Lord. Nimrod was the founder of this city which
later became Babylon. His reputation is found in
verse 8 where it is said that he was a "mighty one
in the earth." Verse 9 goes on to say that he was
"the mighty hunter before the Lord."

In the same passage a little bit later on we
find this description of Babel:

> *Therefore is the name of it called Babel;*
> *because the LORD did there confound the*
> *language of all the earth: and from thence*
> *did the LORD scatter them abroad upon*
> *the face of all the earth.* Genesis 11:9

These verses give us the keys to start
unlocking the "Mystery Babylon," also called
"The mother of harlots." The first mention finds
her being judged of the Lord because she is man's
mightiest attempt to reach heaven without God.

She was man's challenge to God. Therefore God scattered all of her citizens throughout the world and divided their languages. Every country, every city, and every village can trace its roots to Babel.

The first time we find the word Babylon, it is used as an adjective defining worldly things that one of God's people was coveting after. The consequence for his covetousness was the death of him and his family.

> *When I saw among the spoils a goodly <u>Babylonish</u> garment, and two hundred shekels of silver, and a wedge of gold of fifty shekels weight, then I coveted them, and took them; and, behold, they are hid in the earth in the midst of my tent, and the silver under it.* Joshua 7:21

Daniel Chapter 2 describes Babylon as a world empire. Nebuchadnezzar's kingdom was the head of gold. Next came the Media-Persia Empire which were represented by the breast and arms of silver. The belly and thighs of brass illustrated the Grecian Empire, then came the legs of iron which were the Roman Empire. Finally came the feet that were part iron and part clay. Those feet are interesting because they are a mixture of the Roman Empire and something quite a bit inferior, and they end up divided into 10 different kingdoms. That final kingdom is the one we are living in now. The font I am using to type this text is called "Times New Roman." The numbers that are used to divide this text into its parts are called "Roman numerals." The date that was used to copyright this book

was taken from a Roman-based calendar. The days
of the week are named after Roman gods. All of
the European languages including ours, are based
on Latin, which is the Roman language. The reli-
gious system recognized as the most powerful in
the world is called the Roman Catholic Church.
Our Republican-Democratic system finds its roots
in Roman politics. The senate comes straight out
of the Roman governing system.

You see, the entire world system of governing itself without God is Babylon. It is the entire effort of man to show God that He is not
needed in the affairs of man. That is why Babylon
will fall. And that fall will be a great fall.

III. Identifying a Spiritual Truth

A. Walk in the Spirit—
Success in the Christian life depends on
whether you walk in the Spirit. This is explained
quite plainly by the apostle Paul in both Romans
Chapter 8 and Galatians Chapter 5. But what does
this mean? Let's see if the first mention principle
will help us.

God is the first one to walk in the Bible.
Genesis 3:8 finds Him walking in the Garden of
Eden. Genesis 5:22, and 24 tell us that Enoch
walked with God. Genesis 6:9 says the same about
Noah—that he walked with God.

The first command to walk is given to
Abraham in Genesis 13:14-18. The promise to

Abraham is that all of the ground he walks on will be his possession. Can you see the spiritual lesson? That you will have spiritual possession in direct correlation to how much ground you cover while walking in the Spirit?

In this same context of the Lord's command to Abraham to walk, we find another interesting clue. In Genesis 17:1 the Lord tells Abraham, *I am the Almighty God; walk before me, and be thou perfect.* This walking then has to do with position as well as possession. Your walking must be done before the Lord. The Spirit will never lead you to walk away from the presence of the Lord.

B. Righteousness—

The first time this word "righteousness" appears is in Genesis 15:6. It is in the same verse that we find the words "believed" and "counted" for the first time.

This gives us the mind of God on the only way in which righteousness is imputed. Righteousness will never come by good works. If you believe, then you will be counted righteous.

Subsequent Mention Principle

I.   Names of Key Players
II. Spiritual Warfare not revealed before
III. Facts about the Prophets and Patriarchs
IV. Events not Previously Recorded
V.   About Angels

chapter TEN

The Subsequent Mention Principle

God, who at sundry times and in divers manners
spake in time past unto the fathers by the prophets...
Hebrews 1:1

The principle by which later Scripture adds details of prior events, or gives events never before recorded.

I. Names of key players in Scripture

Sometimes there will be people who are involved in certain events that are not specifically named in an immediate passage. Maybe they are described in a group (ie., a family or a group of brothers.) But then somewhere later in Scripture they are specifically named.

An example is found in the story of the magicians in Egypt who were drawn into the contest with Moses. It is not until II Timothy 3:8 that we find their names, Jannes and Jambres.

II. Spiritual warfare not revealed before

Job describes to us a warfare that was going on in the spiritual realms that we cannot see. The book of Daniel also records such an event when the angel was to deliver a message to Daniel and was held up for 21 days. However, we are not given a look at the spiritual warfare side of the story every time.

Sometimes, though, you might find a glimpse of it later—as in Jude 9 where we find Michael disputing with Satan over the body of Moses.

II Peter 2:4 also mentions another event that was heretofore covered. It says that there were "the angels that sinned" who are kept in chains reserved for judgment.

I Peter 3:18-19 gives us an interesting view of what happened when Jesus was in the grave for three days.

III. Facts about the prophets and patriarchs

In Jude 14 we are told that Enoch, the seventh from Adam, was a prophet who foretold the coming judgment on the earth, and his sermon outline is given.

II Peter 2:5 explains to us that Noah was not just a boat builder, but that he also was "a preacher of righteousness."

A surprise is found in II Peter 2: 6-8 when Lot is described as "just Lot," "that righteous man" having a "righteous soul." The Old Testament account gives no suggestion of this.

Jonah was swallowed by a great fish that God had especially prepared. It is not until Matthew 12:40 that we find out this was a whale that was actually prepared on the fifth day of creation.

IV. Events not previously recorded

Revelation 2:14 records the teachings of Balaam and Balac.

Hebrews 9:19 speaks of a specific sprinkling of blood was not recorded in Exodus.

The book of I Kings says nothing about Elijah praying that it might not rain. This fact is added to the story only in James 5:17.

V. About Angels

Although we know about other beings early on in the Bible, it isn't until later that names and positions are explained. Michael the archangel and some of his work is described in Daniel 10:13 and Jude 9.

It is in Genesis 3 that we first find out about someone who is in conflict with God, and he had the power to possess a serpent. But it is not until Isaiah 14:12-14 that Lucifer's original position and goals are explained.

Full Mention Principle

I.   Justification
II.   Love
III.   The Mystery of the Church
IV.   The Resurrection
V.   The Restoration of Israel
VI.   The Tongue
VII.   The Gift of Tongues
VIII. Governmental Authority
IX.   Works
X.   The Anti-Christ
XI.   The Marriage of the Lamb
XII.   The Completeness of the Word
XIII. The Trinity

chapter *ELEVEN*

The Full Mention Principle

And to make all men see what is the fellowship of
the mystery, which from the beginning
of the world hath been hid in God,
who created all things by Jesus Christ...
Ephesians 3:9

This principle states that somewhere in His Word, God will take the scattered fragments regarding a particular truth that is important and summarize it in a concise way.

A gold prospector who stumbles onto a vein of gold hopes that the direction he is following the vein will take him to the mother lode or the main source of the gold. So it is with the Bible student. Follow the veins of truth and they will take you to the heart of the subject. It is there you will find that truth described in a complete and concise way.

> *Somewhere in His Word, God will assemble the scattered fragments of a particular truth in a concise way.*

I. Justification

The entire Bible teaches Justification by faith alone. It is in Romans 5, however, that it is explained clearly enough for even the Catholic priest, Martin Luther, to understand.

II. Love

Jesus said that the greatest commandment is to love God with all our being, and the second greatest commandment is to love our neighbors as ourselves. Several times He states that the greatest kind of love is to lay down your life for others. A full description of how to love is found in I Corinthians 13. This is considered the "mother lode" on the subject of love.

III. The Mystery of the Church

The Apostle Paul seemed to have the greatest grasp on the mystery of the Church. Even Peter recognized this fact in II Peter 3:15-16. The book of Ephesians is where we find it explained the best. Ephesians chapter 1 describes the seal of the Spirit. Ephesians chapter 2 tells us about the unifying of the Gentile and Jewish believers. Ephesians chapter 3 reveals that church was in the mind of God before the foundations of the world. Ephesians chapter 4 explains how the church is organized. Ephesians chapter 5 commands us how to conduct ourselves in our relationships. Ephesians chapter 6 identifies the purpose of the church.

IV. The Resurrection

I Corinthians 15 gives us the clearest outline of the resurrection and its vital importance in the heart of the Gospel message. It is here that the resurrection of Christ is validated and He is identified as the "firstfruits" of the resurrection. It is in this chapter also that the apostle takes the time to explain the difference between a terrestrial body and a celestial body.

V. Restoration of Israel

Romans 11 spells out God's plan for the restoration of the nation of Israel.

VI. The Tongue

James 3 spends a lot of time on the subject of the tongue. It takes all of the concepts given throughout the Bible and wraps them up into a neat little package, explaining the power and the danger of this little member.

VII. The Gift of Tongues

The Bible mentions the gift of tongues several times. I Corinthians 12-14 describes it as the tongues of men and of angels, indicating that there are two different types of this gift. There is the language of men, which is natural and explainable. But there is also the supernatural gift of tongues, termed "the tongue of angels." The lode passage on this subject is found in Acts 2. This is where the complete explanation can be found.

VIII. Obedience to Governmental Authority

Romans 13 gives the most concise statement of God's opinion on the role of the government in our lives. It is here we learn that human authorities are actually minister of God, and we are to obey them as such.

IX. Works

James 2 is the mother lode of truth on the subject of works and its role in the life of the Christian.

X.   The Coming of the Anti-Christ

The Scriptures hint at the coming of a specific person we call the Anti-Christ. II Thessalonians 2 is the passage that seems to give us the clearest picture of what he will be like.

XI.   The Marriage of the Lamb

Revelation 21 is the chapter that describes to us the marriage of the Lamb. Before you build your opinions concerning Eschatology, you should do a thorough study on this chapter.

XII. The Completeness of the Word of God

Revelation 22:18-19 cannot be called the only word on the completeness of God's Word, but it can be called the final word on it. It is here that most people will go to prove that the Scriptures should not be tampered with.

XIII. The Trinity

We are first introduced to the Trinity in Genesis chapter 1. God said "Let us make man in our image." In the baptism of Jesus we see three different personalities immerge, but it isn't until we get to I John 5:7 that the Three-in –One concept is explained.

The Application Principle

I.   The Mystical Method
II. The Allegorical Method
III. The Rationalism Method
IV. The Apologetic Method
V.   The Literal Method
VI. The Inductive Method

chapter TWELVE

The Application Principle

For whatsoever things were written
aforetime were written for our learning,
that we through patience and comfort of the
scriptures might have hope.
Romans 15:4

This principle has been defined as *The princi-ple by which an application of truth may be made only after the correct interpretation has been learned.*

Applying the truth of the Scriptures to our lives is important. ***Misapplication*** is easy if you are looking for the applause of man. I Timothy 3:6 warns us against falling into the condemnation of the Devil. This warning would not be there unless it were a very real danger. ***Sectarianism*** will cloud your judgment. In other words, you can be swayed by denominational pressure to misinterpret a scrip-ture. You can believe something just because it was what you were taught without actually having any Biblical grounds. Many Buddhists believe what they were taught, but their doctrine will not produce salvation.

Good common sense is needed to apply Scripture.

And they shall teach my people the difference between the holy and profane, and cause them to discern between the unclean and the clean.   Ezekiel 44:23

Study, that is, good mental industry, is needed.

Till I come, give attendance to reading, to exhortation, to doctrine. Neglect not the gift that is in thee, which was given thee by prophecy, with the laying on of the hands of the presbytery. Meditate upon these things; give thyself wholly to them; that thy profiting may appear to all. Take heed unto thyself, and unto the doctrine; continue in them: for in doing this thou shalt both save thyself, and them that hear thee.
                    I Timothy 4:13-16

There are six different methods of application. Each one needs to be considered with care. Depending on the context, sometimes one application might apply, and sometimes another.

I. Mystical Method

Sometimes there are mysteries that are simply mentioned in the Bible and cannot be understood by common interpretation. A good example of this would be the image in Daniel Chapter Two. Nebuchadnezzar did not understand the mystical nuances of the dream and therefore tried to build a matching image in the middle of the plain. If he had used this method of application, Shadrach, Meshach, and Abednego would never have entered the flames of the furnace.

II. Allegorical Method

The parables of Christ are intended to be applied allegorically. They are stories with hidden truth.

And the disciples came, and said unto him, Why speakest thou unto them in parables? He answered and said unto them, Because it is given unto you to know the mysteries of the kingdom of heaven, but to them it is not given. For whosoever hath, to him shall be given, and he shall have more abundance: but whosoever hath not, from him shall be taken away even that he hath. Therefore speak I to them in parables: because they seeing see not; and hearing they hear not, neither do they understand. Matthew 13:10-13

Many times truths can be illustrated by a story in the Old Testament. Paul, himself, said that they were written for our learning. The story of the sacrifice of Isaac is a classic example of this. The Bible tells us that Abraham told Isaac that God would "provide himself, a lamb" (Genesis 22:8). This is an obvious picture of the sacrifice of Christ with an interesting twist. A ram, the father of a lamb, is found in the thicket as the substitutionary sacrifice.

Be careful not to build doctrines with the allegorical method. It is important to use it only for the purpose of illustrating an already established doctrine.

III. Rationalism Method

You will often find that the commandments of God are very logical. It is quite possible to explain much of God's truth with mathematical formulas and equations. The book of Hebrews is a beautiful example of this method. The writer of Hebrews started with what the Jews were familiar with and then step by step led them down an intellectual path that ended with Jesus Christ.

> *Correct application can only be made after correct interpretation.*

Every scriptural truth cannot be explained this way, however. Be careful not to fit an Infinite God into the thinking process of finite man.

IV. Apologetic Method

Sometimes a passage needs to be studied piece by piece. This method maintains that every statement in a given passage is truth.

For precept must be upon precept, precept upon precept; line upon line, line upon line; here a little, and there a little:
Isaiah 28:10

When you see every line as containing truth, and then you meditate on those individual truths, you can learn much.

V. Literal Method

Taking the Word of God at face value is called the Literal Method of Application. The Bible says, *If a man have long hair, it is a shame.* There is no need to look any deeper for a hidden meaning. The Bible says, *And be not drunk with wine, wherein is excess.* It literally means don't get drunk. The Bible says, *Children, obey your parents.* The Bible says, *Lie not one to another.* The Bible says, *Be sure your sin will find you out.* These are all very simple statements and very easy to understand. There is no hidden meaning – no sequence of logical thoughts – no mystical nuances. It is the straightforward truth with no need for interpretation.

VI. Inductive Method

The Bible is a single unit with the same truths often stated again and again using different methods of presentation. When you want to know about a particular issue or subject, collect all of the Bible verses on the subject and read them all. Let the facts speak for themselves. This is what we call the inductive method.

How do you know which one of these methods to use?

• <u>Common sense</u>
  In most cases common sense will direct you on which application to use.

• <u>Questions</u>
  Asking the following questions will help you to determine the method of application to use.
    a. Who is speaking?
    b. Who is being spoken to?
    c. What actions were taken by those who heard the command?
    d. What kind of action is possible for me to take?

• <u>Testing</u>
  Test the methods that appear to be the proper ones and see what the results are. If your conclusions coincide with the basic direction of the Word of God, than you are probably on the right track. Use these three perspectives when you are testing
    1. Primary Interpretation - There will be the perspective of those to whom the passage is addressed. What it meant to them is the primary interpretation.
    2. Practical Application - This deals with how the passage can relate to you and your situation.

3. Prophetical Revelation - Often there is a hidden prophesy or application that can be taken from an otherwise obscure passage.

- <u>Prayer</u>

Ask God to direct your understanding according to His promise. God does not try to hide His will from us. If you choose to look for His guidance - He will give it to you.

> *If any of you lack wisdom, let him ask of God, that giveth to all men liberally, and upbraideth not; and it shall be given him.* James 1:5

- <u>Yield</u>

Expect the Holy Spirit to teach you as Christ promised.

> *Howbeit when he, the Spirit of truth, is come, he will guide you into all truth: for he shall not speak of himself; but whatsoever he shall hear, that shall he speak: and he will shew you things to come.* John 16:13

The Consequence Principle

I.   Naming Babel
II.   Protecting Abimelech
III.   Protecting the Hebrew midwives
IV.   The reason for some drastic instructions
V.   The reason Jerusalem was not destroyed
VI.   The writer explains a comment of Christ
VII.   The action that produced fish
VIII.   The result of the promises of God
IX.   A friend of the world
X.   The reason the world acts the way it does

chapter THIRTEEN

The Consequence Principle

Wherein God, willing more abundantly to
shew unto the heirs of promise the immutability
of his counsel, confirmed it by an oath...
Hebrews 6:17

Sometimes God will explain the reasons for a particular command or action just before or after He gives it. This is known as the Consequence Principle. You can find these reasons whenever the words "Wherefore" or "Therefore" appear. Someone once described this principle this way: "Whenever you see the word 'therefore' in the Bible, look to see what it's there for."

> *Whenever you find the word "therefore" in the Bible, look to see what it is there for.*

Interestingly enough, these words can be found 1,585 times in Scripture. It is awe inspiring to know that God wants us to understand his reasons for doing things.

The following verses are just a few examples of the different ways in which God will explain Himself. The underlined portion of the verse is God's reason for the action in the rest of the verse.

The first verse here tells us that God called the city "Babel." The underlined portion of the verse tells us why He called it that.

> ***Therefore*** *is the name of it called Babel;* <u>*because the LORD did there confound the language of all the earth: and from thence did the LORD scatter them abroad upon the face of all the earth.*</u>   Genesis 11:9

In this verse God is explaining to Abimelech just why He protected him from doing something that would have resulted in judgment.

> *And* <u>*God said unto him in a dream, Yea, I know that thou didst this in the integrity of thy heart; for I also withheld thee from sinning against me*</u>*:* ***therefore*** *suffered I thee not to touch her.*   Genesis 20:6

Here we find God's protection over the Hebrew midwives in Egypt, because of their refusal to abort the Hebrew babies as the Pharaoh had commanded them.

> <u>*And the midwives said unto Pharaoh, Because the Hebrew women are not as the Egyptian women; for they are lively, and are delivered ere the midwives come in*</u>

unto them. **Therefore** *God dealt well with the midwives: and the people multiplied, and waxed very mighty.* Exodus 1:19-20

Some drastic action was taken in this passage of scripture. Moses, the man of God, commanded that some of the children of Israel kill certain of their captives. The reason for this drastic undertaking is underlined.

And Moses was wroth with the officers of the host, with the captains over thousands, and captains over hundreds, which came from the battle. And Moses said unto them, Have ye saved all the women alive? Behold, these caused the children of Israel, through the counsel of Balaam, to commit trespass against the LORD in the matter of Peor, and there was a plague among the congregation of the LORD. *Now* **therefore** *kill every male among the little ones, and kill every woman that hath known man by lying with him.* Numbers 31:14-17

In this verse God explains why He did not keep His promise to destroy Jerusalem.

And when the LORD saw that they humbled themselves, the word of the LORD came to Shemaiah, saying, They have humbled themselves; **therefore** *I will not destroy them, but I will grant them some deliverance; and my wrath shall not be poured out upon Jerusalem by the hand of Shishak.* II Chronicles 12:7

This time God explains why He said what He did. Jesus made a statement that we would otherwise not understand, so He put the explanation of His comment before a "therefore."

For he knew who should betray him; **therefore** *said he, Ye are not all clean.*

John 13:11

John relates the miracle of the full fish net. The disciples had fished all night and caught nothing. Jesus appeared and gave them a command to cast the net on the other side, which command they followed and consequently filled their net with fishes.

And he said unto them, Cast the net on the right side of the ship, and ye shall find. They cast **therefore***, and now they were not able to draw it for the multitude of fishes.*

John 21:6

Not only does God give us reasons for His actions, but in some cases the words "therefore" and "wherefore" are used to explain why we should take certain actions. Paul gives us one such example in the following verse:

Having **therefore** *these promises, dearly beloved, let us cleanse ourselves from all filthiness of the flesh and spirit, perfecting holiness in the fear of God.*

II Corinthians 7:1

In this verse the Apostle Paul explains his own outlook on life. God had given him a promise that was all Paul needed to sustain him through the trial he faced.

> *And he said unto me, My grace is sufficient for thee: for my strength is made perfect in weakness. Most gladly **therefore** will I rather glory in my infirmities, that the power of Christ may rest upon me.*
>
>   II Corinthians 12:9

In this verse a verdict is pronounced on those who are a friend of the world. The explanation given is that this verdict is a consequence of a natural law.

> *Ye adulterers and adulteresses, know ye not that the friendship of the world is enmity with God? whosoever **therefore** will be a friend of the world is the enemy of God.*   James 4:4

Our last example of this principle explains why the world does what it does.

> *They are of the world: **therefore** speak they of the world, and the world heareth them.*   I John 4:5

The Principles of Prophecy

I. The Three Subjects of Bible Prophecy
  A. Gentiles
  B. Israel
  C. Church
II. The Seven Issues of O.T. Prophets
  A. The prophet's own day
  B. The 70 - year captivity
  C. The restoration of Israel
  D. The coming of Messiah
  E. The worldwide dispersion
  F. The Great Tribulation
  G. The Kingdom of Messiah on this earth
III. The Double Reference
  A. Immanuel—Emanuel
  B. Joshua—Jesus
  C. Pentecost—Tribulation/Millennium
IV. The Three Prophetical Eras
  A. Pre-Exilic
  B. Exilic
  C. Post-Exilic
V. Interpretation of Prophecy
  A. The prophet's interpretation
  B. The facts of history
  C. Inspiration
  D. The prophecy itself
  E. Some prophecies are closed

chapter *FOURTEEN*

The Principles of Prophecy

Of which salvation the prophets have in-
quired and searched diligently,
who prophesied of the grace
that should come unto you:
I Peter 1:10

Prophecy is an intriguing part of Scripture, and many have fallen into the trap of trying to second-guess God. The best interpretation of prophecy is history. Often there are things described by a prophet which he cannot even comprehend because he has nothing with which to compare it. For example, consider how Daniel would have described an airplane, or how Joel would have described a tank, or how John would have described a computer. This causes speculation on the part of the Bible student and can lead to misinterpretation. The quickest way to embarrassment is to build a prophetical theory on speculation.

While prophecy can often be quite elusive to

us, there are some basic principles that can be used unerringly to help guide us through its potential quicksand.

I. The Three Subjects of Bible Prophecy

A. The Called-Out People – The Gentiles

Noah and his family were the first group of people separated from the world. Don't forget that the Gentile nations are all descendants of Noah, the faithful preacher of righteousness.

B. The Called-Out Race – Israel

Soon after the tower of Babel and the confusing of the languages. God separated out yet another man named Abraham. He was the father of the Hebrew nation. Old Testament prophecy deals predominately with this nation because those prophets were Hebrew. The book of Daniel is the exception, dealing almost exclusively with the Gentile nations. The original text was written in three different languages.

C. The Called-Out Kingdom – The Church

The Old Testament alludes to the Church (Daniel 2:35,45 / I Peter 2:3-8) but is misunderstood by the prophets because they cannot relate to it.

Where is America? America is considered a Gentile nation and will be treated as such, according to the Bible. Our pride insists that, surely as great a nation as we are, we should be mentioned somewhere in the Bible. This is not necessarily so. We are only a little over 200 years old and are already self-destructing. My hope is that we will be found faithful in Matt. 25:31-46 and Revelation 21:24-26. Maybe if there are 10 righteous....

II. The Seven Issues of the O.T. Prophets

There were seven particular issues that seemed to occupy the minds and hearts of the Old Testament prophets. You will find that most of their prophecies will fall into one of these categories. These are sometimes called the 7 heads of prophecy.

        A. The prophet's own day
        B. The 70–year captivity
        C. The restoration of Israel
        D. The coming of Messiah
        E. The worldwide dispersion
        F. The Great Tribulation
        G. The Kingdom of Messiah on this earth

III. The Double Reference

Sometimes the Holy Spirit will use a particular passage to refer to an incident close to the prophet, but it will also be a prophecy of something in the future.

        A. Immanuel - Emmanuel Isaiah 7:14

This was a prophecy concerning the birth of the son of Isaiah, but Matthew 1:23 states that it was also a prediction of the birth of Christ.

        B. Joshua - Jesus Deuteronomy 18:18

This was a promise to Moses that there would be a leader after him that would lead the people to the Lord. The capital letter on the word Prophet tells us that the promise also has something to do with a specific person in the future. This is a clue that points to Christ.

      C. Pentecost – Tribulation/Millennium
             Joel 2:28-32

      The prophecy by the prophet Joel is pointing to the end of the world. However, Peter, under the influence of the Holy Spirit, states that Pentecost is also a fulfillment of this prophecy.

IV. The Three Prophetical Eras

      The Prophets in the Old Testament wrote in three specific time periods. They were as follows:

      A. Pre-exilic   - There were 11 prophets who prophesied before the 70-year captivity, otherwise known as "the exile."

             In Judah (Southern tribes, Benjamin and Judah) –

                Isaiah, Micah, Nahum

             In Israel (Northern 10 tribes) -

                Jonah, Amos, Hosea

    -Silence for 70 years-

             In Judah –

                Habakkuk, Zephaniah, Jeremiah

             In Israel –

                Joel, Obadiah

      B. Exilic – There were only three prophets who prophesied during the exile. Notice that they are all from Judah. Jeremiah prophesied both before and during the exile.

             In Judah –

                Ezekiel, Daniel, Jeremiah

    -Silence for 14 years-

C. Post-exilic – These were the prophets who came after the exile. Notice that sometimes their prophecies are identical to those of the pre-exilic prophets.

In Judah –

Haggai, Zechariah

- Silence for 29 years-

In Judah –

Malachi

V. Interpretation of Prophecy

The interpretation of Prophecy can be somewhat illusive. However, we have listed here some guides that might keep you on the right course.

A. The prophet sometimes gives his own interpretation.   Ezekiel 37:1-14

B. The facts of history give interpretation. Jeremiah 32:7-8

C. Inspiration gives interpretation. Acts 2:25-31

D. The prophecy sometimes is its own interpreter.   Acts 1:9-11

E. There are some prophecies are not open to us.   Daniel 12:8-13, Revelation 10:4

The Divine Will
In Revelation Principle

I.   In the Beginning God
II.   The Body of Moses
III.   Noah's Drunkenness
IV.   David's Sin
V.   The Trinity
VI.   The Hypostatic Union of Christ
VII.   The Life in the Blood
VIII.   Where did Lazarus go?

chapter FIFTEEN

The Divine Will
In Revelation Principle

*How that he was caught up into paradise,
and heard unspeakable words, which it
is not lawful for a man to utter.*
II Corinthians 12:4

This is the principle in which we understand that God will disclose to us what He wants us to understand. God does not always explain His actions to us. Sometimes He reveals things that we would not have discovered on our own, and sometimes He will *not* reveal things that we would like to know.

We must realize that some matters are of God's domain and His alone.

I. *In the beginning God...*

God begins His book with the supposition that there is a God. There is no explanation of where God came from. That is for Him to know, and not for us.

II The Body of Moses

God buried Moses in a place that only He knows. God chose not to reveal the location of Moses' grave to man. We find out later in Jude that Satan and Michael were fighting over the body of Moses, but we don't know why or where. It is safely assumed that the mystery of the burial place of Moses was to keep man from worshiping Moses as a idol. It is theorized that the fight for Moses' body was so that Moses could return as one of the two witnesses in Revelation.

> *God will tell us only what He wants us to Understand.*

III Noah's Drunkenness

This is a fact that any other biographer would have left out. Up to this point there is an awe about Noah and his relationship to God.

IV David's Sin

God doesn't hide from our sin. He promises that our sin will certainly find us out. After David's mighty victories, we are amazed by his mighty wickedness. Yet God still calls David the "apple of *His* eye."

V The Trinity

The Bible reveals to us that God is a three-in-one being. But we have no real explanation of this fact. We are only to believe it. God has chosen to conceal some of the facts of this triune existence.

VI The Hypostatic Union of Christ

This is simply a fancy name to describe the two natures of Christ. Exactly how Jesus could be both man and God is beyond our understanding. God in His Divine Will chose to tell us about it without giving us the understanding we desire.

VII The Life is in the Blood

This is a statement made to Noah. We know that life cannot exist without blood, but neither can it exist without air, or food, or water. What exactly is meant here is beyond us. Of course, there is an allegorical teaching about the blood of Christ, but scientifically speaking we don't understand it completely.

VIII Where did Lazarus go?

When Lazarus was dead for four days, where was he? In paradise? Did he know he was dead? The body was dead, but where was the spirit and soul of Lazarus? There is no answer given. That is God's business, not ours.

The Human Willingness Principle

I. Illumination does not depend upon the teacher.
   A. Peter vs. Judas
   B. Respect for a teacher
II. Illumination comes while you are doing the will of God.
   A. Discernment
   B. His Truth in us
III. Illumination comes when you hunger for it.
   A. Hunger for the right thing
   B. Hunger is a motivator

chapter *SIXTEEN*

The Human Willingness Principle

Howbeit when he, the Spirit of truth, is come, he will guide you into all truth: for he shall not speak of himself; but whatsoever he shall hear, that shall he speak: and he will shew you things to come.   John 16:13

This principle reminds us that God's truth is guaranteed to willing souls. If you desire illumination, you can have it. Matthew 7:7 says, *Ask, and it shall be given you; seek, and ye shall find; knock, and it shall be opened unto you...*

I. Illumination does not depend upon the teacher.

A. The Holy Spirit taught Peter but not Judas (Matthew 16:16 -17). Jesus is a Master Teacher. Isn't it interesting that Judas did not learn? Understanding does not always depend on the skill of the teacher. Most of the time it de-

> *If you desire illumination you can have it!*

pends on the willingness of the student.

B. Truth is not determined by what you have been taught. You may respect the teacher. You may be impressed by the teacher's life, but that does not mean that what you are being taught is truth. There are many religions that illustrate this point.

II. Illumination comes while you are doing the will of God.

A. In John 7:17 Jesus explains to us that if we will do the will of God we will know whether doctrine is good or bad.

B. Again John tells us in I John 2:4-5 that if we do the will of God, His truth will be in us.

III. Illumination comes when you are hungering for it.

A. Hunger after the right thing. What are you hungry for? Do you want to know righteousness in your life? Matthew 5:6 tells us that if we hunger for righteousness, we will be filled with it.

B. Hunger causes motivation for filling. If we are hungry for something, we will be motivated to go after it. Matthew 5:6.

The Progressive Revelation Principle

I.   The Sixth Commandment
II. The Trinity
III. The Lamb of God

chapter *SEVENTEEN*

The Progressive Revelation Principle

...Which in other ages was not made known unto the sons of men, as it is now revealed unto his holy apostles and prophets by the Spirit... Ephesians 3:5

Of which salvation the prophets have enquired and searched diligently, who prophesied of the grace that should come unto you... 1 Peter 1:10

Truths that are introduced in the first book of the Bible become clearer as the Word proceeds. As in any book, details are added as the story progresses. Here we have listed three examples of this principle.

I. The Sixth Commandment— "Thou Shalt not kill"

A. The first time we are introduced to killing is in Genesis 4:1-16. It is obvious that the motivation for the killing was rebellion to God and misplaced anger.

B. In the Decalogue the commandment is spelled out clearly for the first time. Exodus 20:13

C. Numbers 35:16 describes a murderer.

D. God tells the Israelites to kill the inhabitants of Jericho. Joshua 6:17

E. God tells them to kill the Sodomites. Leviticus 20:13

F. God makes allowances for vengeance killing. Numbers 35

G. God tells them not to kill their babies at Molech. Leviticus 18:21

H. David has Joab killed for shedding "the blood of war" in a time of peace. I Kings 2:5 -6

I. Jesus explains to us that the Devil was a murderer from the beginning. John 8:44

J. John tell us that if we hate our brother we are a murderer. I John 3:15

Obviously, a comprehensive study of this commandment cannot be done here. However, you can see that tracing the subject through the Bible will not lead you to pacifism.

II The Trinity

A. The Hebrew word for God found in the first verse of the Bible is *Elohim.* Genesis 1:1. The interesting thing about this word is that the first part "El" is a singular word, but the last part "him" is a plural suffix. In Hebrew there is a singular tense meaning one, there is dual tense meaning two, and there is plural tense meaning three or more. The "him" suffix is a plural tense meaning three or more.

B. The next time we get a peek at this concept is

in Genesis 1:26 when God said, *Let us make man in our image, after our likeness...* A study of the angels will lead us to conclude that He was not speaking to them. The only one He could have been addressing was Himself (see Isaiah 45:5-6).

C. At the baptism of Jesus (Matthew 3:16-17) there is a clear picture of the Three Persons. There is the Father's voice from heaven, the Spirit descending like a dove, and the Son standing in the water.

D. John 1:1-14 describes the "Word," who is understood to be Jesus Christ by John's testimony, as being one with God the Creator.

E. It is not until I John 5:7 that it is explained specifically what is going on. *For there are three that bear record in heaven, the Father, the Word, and the Holy Ghost: and these three are one.*

III The Lamb of God

A. The first sacrifice is found in Genesis 3:21. God makes coats of skin to cover the results of the sin of Adam and Eve. There is no direct reference to an animal sacrifice although it is an obvious deduction that animals had to die to produce the skins.

B. Abel's lamb found in Genesis 4 is recognized by God as the only acceptable offering. This is the first clear statement that a lamb was necessary for atonement.

C. Gen. 22 adds to our understanding of the

sacrificial Lamb when Isaac is replaced on the altar with a substitutionary offering.

D. We then learn in Leviticus 16 that the sacrificial Lamb has two duties – to live and to die.

E. A shocking detail is added in Isaiah 53. It is in this passage that the Lamb is introduced to us as a Man.

F. The Man, Jesus, is the Lamb of God that takes away the sin of the world.   John 1:29

G. Jesus is the Lamb of Isaiah 53.   Acts 8

H. The sacrifice of Jesus the Lamb was enough to pay for all of the sins of the world.
The book of Hebrews

I. The Lamb is the Lion of the Tribe of Judah.
The book of Revelation

The Illustrative Principle

I.   Lying to the Holy Ghost
II. Thou shalt not covet
III. The angels that sinned
IV. Wicked imaginations
V.   Sodomy

chapter *EIGHTEEN*

The Illustrative Principle

Now these things were our examples,
to the intent we should not lust after
evil things, as they also lusted.
I Corinthians 10:6

Sometimes God will illustrate His displeasure with a certain sin by executing judgment in a particular case. It is important to understand this principle, lest you think that God is inconsistent in His judgments. Oftentimes He makes strong statements to us by judging a life. His purpose is not to set a precedent, but rather to illustrate His opinion.

I. Lying to the Holy Ghost
Acts 5 – Ananias and Saphira
This passage points out that fear fell on the whole church. If there was no sin, there would be no fear. The presence of fear indicates there might have been others that were contemplating

this kind of sin.

II. *Thou shalt not covet*
I Kings 21 - God used Ahab's covetousness for Naboth's vineyard to illustrate the wickedness of this sin, as well as the consequences.

III. *The angels that sinned*
Peter tells us in II Peter 2:4 that the angels that were cast out of heaven are supposed to be viewed as examples.

> *God is not inconsistent in His judgments.*

IV. Wicked imaginations
In Genesis Chapter 6 we see God's wrath visited on those who have wicked imaginations.

V. Sodomy
Genesis 19 - Some folks in our culture would have us believe that Sodomy is a normal alternative lifestyle. God's comment to that is an entire culture completely obliterated by fire and brimstone.

The Law of Repetition Principle

I.   For Emphasis
II. For Explanation
III. For Perspective

chapter NINETEEN

The Law of Repetition Principle

For God speaketh once, yea twice, yet man
perceiveth it not...Then he openeth the ears of men,
and sealeth their instruction, That he may withdraw
man from his purpose, and hide pride from man.
Job 33:14

This is when God repeats some truth or subject already given, generally with the addition of details not given before.

I. Sometimes repetition is for the purpose of emphasis.

Notice the underlined phrases. Three times Jesus makes exactly the same statement to emphasize a very strong message.

And whosoever shall offend one of these
little ones that believe in me, it is better for
him that a millstone were hanged about his
neck, and he were cast into the sea. And if
thy hand offend thee, cut it off: it is better

*for thee to enter into life maimed, than
having two hands to go into hell, into the
fire that never shall be quenched:* **<u>Where
their worm dieth not, and the fire is not
quenched</u>**. *And if thy foot offend thee, cut
it off: it is better for thee to enter halt into
life, than having two feet to be cast into
hell, into the fire that never shall be
quenched:* **<u>Where their worm dieth not,
and the fire is not quenched</u>**. *And if thine
eye offend thee, pluck it out: it is better for
thee to enter into the kingdom of God with
one eye, than having two eyes to be cast
into hell fire:* **<u>Where their worm dieth not,
and the fire is not quenched</u>**.

Mark 9:42-48

II. Sometimes repetition is for the purpose of explanation.

Here we see something that David said in the
Psalms repeated in the New Testament by the
Apostle Peter. He is explaining the meaning of the
passage.

*Therefore my heart is glad, and my glory
rejoiceth: my flesh also shall rest in hope.
For* **<u>thou wilt not leave my soul in hell;
neither wilt thou suffer thine Holy One to
see corruption.</u>** *Thou wilt shew me the
path of life: in thy presence is fulness of
joy; at thy right hand there are pleasures
for evermore.*   Psalm 16:9-11

Men and brethren, let me freely speak unto you of the patriarch David, that he is both dead and buried, and his sepulchre is with us unto this day. Therefore being a prophet, and knowing that God had sworn with an oath to him, that of the fruit of his loins, according to the flesh, he would raise up Christ to sit on his throne; **_He seeing this before spake of the resurrection of Christ, that his soul was not left in hell, neither his flesh did see corruption._** *This Jesus hath God raised up, whereof we all are witnesses. Therefore being by the right hand of God exalted, and having received of the Father the promise of the Holy Ghost, he hath shed forth this, which ye now see and hear.*   Acts 2:29-33

III. Sometimes repetition is for the purpose of perspective.
    A. The Story of Israel's Kings
        1. The perspective of the **Northern ten tribes** is given in I and II Kings.
        2. The perspective of the **Southern two tribes** is given in I and II Chronicles.
    B. The Life of Christ
        1. Matthew presents Him as the **King of the Jews.**
        2. Mark shows Him as a **Servant.**
        3. Luke paints Him as the **Son of Man.**
        4. John reveals Him as the **Son of God.**

The Numerical Principle

I.   The number of Unity
II.   The number of Division
III.   The number of Divine Holiness
IV.   The number of Creation
V.   The number of Grace
VI.   The number of Man
VII.   The number of Perfection
VIII.   The number of New Beginnings
IX.   The number of Judgment
X.   The number of Divine Completeness
XI.   The number of Incompleteness
XII.   The number of Governmental Perfection
XIII.   The number of Trouble

chapter TWENTY

The Numerical Principle

*Lift up your eyes on high, and behold who hath
created these things, that bringeth out their
host by number: he calleth them all by names
by the greatness of his might, for that he is
strong in power; not one faileth.*
Isaiah 40:26

God places a certain definite meaning on numbers employed by the Holy Spirit in the Scriptures and continues that significance with unbroken uniformity throughout the whole Bible.

There are two Books given to us to explain God:

The Book of God's Word
The Book of God's World

The numerical structure found in God's World (Biology) has a parallel in God's Word (The Bible).

I. The number of Unity

A. The unity of creation
Genesis 1:9 *And God said, Let the waters under the heaven be gathered together unto one place, and let the dry land appear: and it was so.*

B. The unity of man and woman
Genesis 2:21 *And the LORD God caused a deep sleep to fall upon Adam, and he slept: and he took one of his ribs, and closed up the flesh instead thereof...*

C. The unity of the faith
Ephesians 4:4-6 *There is one body, and one Spirit, even as ye are called in one hope of your calling; One Lord, one faith, one baptism, One God and Father of all, who is above all, and through all, and in you all.*

D. The unity of the Godhead
I Timothy 2:5 *For there is one God, and one mediator between God and men, the man Christ Jesus...*
1 John 5:7 *For there are three that bear record in heaven, the Father, the Word, and the Holy Ghost: and these three are one.*

II. The number of Division

A. Day and Night
Genesis 1:16 *And God made two great lights; the greater light to rule the day, and the lesser light to rule the night: he made the stars also.*

B. Male and Female

Matthew 19:4 *And he answered and said unto them, Have ye not read, that he which made them at the beginning made them male and female...*

C. God and Mammon

Matthew 6:24 *No man can serve two masters: for either he will hate the one, and love the other; or else he will hold to the one, and despise the other. Ye cannot serve God and mammon.*

III. The number of Divine Holiness

A. Holy Completion
   Past – Justification
   Present – Transformation
   Future – Glorification
B. Holy Salvation
   Salvation from the Wrath of God
   Salvation from the Bondage of Sin
   Salvation from the Body of Death
C. Holy Action   Matthew 23:23
   Judgment
   Mercy
   Faith
D. Holy Possession   I Corinthians 13:13
   Faith
   Hope
   Charity

IV. The number of Creation

A. 4 directions
North, South, East, West
B. 4 seasons
Summer, Fall, Winter, Spring
C. 4 elements
Earth, Water, Fire, Air

V. The number of Grace

A. David selected 5 stones.
B. Jesus had 5 wounds.
C. There were 5 loaves that fed 5,000.
D. The rich man had 5 brothers that still had
an opportunity.

VI. The number of man

A. 6 sons of Leah
B. 6 days to labor
C. 6 branches on the candlestick
D. Trinity of 6 is the number of the Anti-
Christ.

VII. The perfect number

A. God deals with Israel in periods of 490
years (70x7 - the number of forgiveness).
B. On the 7th day God rested.
"Dr. Stratton says that 6 days out of 7 the
pulse beats faster in the morning and
slower in the evening. On the 7th day it

beats slower in the morning." (pg. 109, *Mastered by the Bible* by Dr. Mark Cambron)

C. 7's enter into the various periods of time it takes for humans and animals to produce their young. A hen - 21 days; duck - 28 days; ostrich and swan - 42 days; rabbit and squirrel - 28 days; cat- 56 days; lion- 35 days; sheep - 147 days; pig - 119 days; cow - 280 days; elephant - 630 days; human species - 280 days *All divisible by 7*

D. 7 walks in Ephesians

E. 7 comings in Thessalonians

F. 7 precious things in I Peter

G. "Mine Hour" 7 times in John

H. 7 Blesseds in Revelation

I. 7 Churches

J. 7 decrees in Daniel

K. "Preacher" 7 times in Ecclesiastes

L. "Jealous God" 7 times in the Old Testament

M. 7 things done by the Good Samaritan

VIII. The number of new beginnings

A. Circumcision on the 8th day

B. David was the 8th son.

C. The 8th day begins a new week.

D. Josiah was 8 when he began to reign.

E. 8 souls were saved in the Flood.

IX. The number of judgment

A. 9 recorded stonings
B. Crucifixion started the 9th hour
C. Abraham was circumcised at 99.
D. Jabin had 900 chariots of iron.
    Judges 4:2,13

X. The number of Divine completeness

A. There are 10 commandments.
B. There were 10 curtains in the tabernacle.
C. There were 10 plagues.
D. Joseph and Joshua both died at 110.
E. 10 men killed Absalom.
F. The Cherubim were 10 cubits high.
G. Our years are 3 score and 10. (The perfect
    number,7, times the complete number, 10.)

XI. The number of incompleteness

A. The last king of Judah reigned 11 years.
    II Chronicles 36:11
B. Jacob had 11 sons before he wrestled with
    God.
C. 11 disciples

XII. The number of governmental perfection

A. 12 tribes of Israel
B. 12 Apostles
C. 12 gates and 12 foundations in the New
    Jerusalem

XIII. The number of trouble (unlucky number)

A. The 13th tribe (Ephraim)
B. Satan appears as a dragon 13 times.
C. Leaven is found 13 times.
D. Ishmael was 13 when God made His covenant with Abram.
E. Solomon spent 13 years building his house.

Important Notes:

There are numerical values to each one of the Hebrew letters. Often times the letters are used in the same way that we might use Roman numerals. Because of this words also have numerical values. There is an entire discipline of study called Gematria which focuses on finding hidden meanings in Hebrew words. Following is a chart identifying the different Hebrew letters and their numerical counterparts.

Letter	Value	Letter	Value
אֿ	1	לֿ	30
בֿ	2	מֿ	40
גֿ	3	נֿ	50
דֿ	4	סֿ	60
הֿ	5	עֿ	70
וֿ	6	פֿ	80
זֿ	7	צֿ	90
חֿ	8	קֿ	100
טֿ	9	רֿ	200
יֿ	10	שֿ	300
כֿ	20	תֿ	400

The Principle of Types

I.   Explaining Types
    A. As a Figure
    B. As a Shadow
    C. As a Part
II. Categorizing Types
    A. Person
    B. Place
    C. Thing
    D. Event
    E. Institution
III. Identifying Types
    A. Repetition in Scripture
    B. Recognition in Scripture

chapter TWENTY-ONE

The Principle of Types

Now all these things happened unto them for ensamples: and they are written for our admonition, upon whom the ends of the world are come.
I Corinthians 10:11

There are divinely anointed illustrations of truth throughout the Scriptures. These are often referred to as "Types." Sometimes a type might be in the form of a person, and sometimes it may be a place, a thing, an event or an institution. Types are not meant to establish doctrine or define it; they are meant to illustrate a truth.

By studying a type you can learn a lot about a specific truth. Remember that each type, however, is merely a shadow of the truth.

Let no man therefore judge you in meat, or in drink, or in respect of an holyday, or of the new moon, or of the Sabbath days: Which are a shadow of things to come; but the body is of Christ. Colossians 2:16-17

*For the law having a shadow of good
things to come, and not the very image of
the things, can never with those sacrifices
which they offered year by year continually
make the comers thereunto perfect.*

Hebrews 10:1

I. Explaining types

The Scriptures themselves have explained to us
the concept of types in many different ways.

A. As a figure
   I Peter 3:21

B. As a shadow
   Hebrews 10:1

C. As a part
   I Corinthians 13:10-12

II. Categorizing types

There are five different categories in which you
can find a "type." The following is a list of these
categories along with a few examples of each:

A. Person
   Isaac– is a type of the Sacrificial Son.
   Moses– is a type of the Intercessory Re-
   deemer.
   Immanuel–is a type of the Virgin Born Son.
   Melchizedek – is a type of the High Priest
   without genealogy.

B. Place
Jerusalem – The city of Peace. A type of the
Eternal Home of the saints
Achor – The door of hope.
A type of the hope of re-
demption

C. Thing
The candlestick – A type
of the church. Revelation
1:12-20
The lamb– A type of
Christ. Isaiah 53.

> *Types are not meant to establish doctrine or define it; they are meant to illustrate truth.*

D. Event
The Exodus– the calling out of the church.
Acts 7:38, I Peter 2:9.
The Jubilee – the redeeming of Israel.

E. Institution
The Priesthood– A type of the work of
Christ.
The Kingship– A type of the reign of Christ.

III Identifying types

The Scripture always has ways to identify
types. The Bible student should never try to establish a type by using his imagination.

A. Repetition in Scripture
Sometimes, through constant repetition, a
pattern will show itself. Such is the case in
the following list where God bypasses the

first and establishes the second. (This is sometimes called "The Special Election Principle.") Clearly we can see a type of the first man, Adam, and the role of the second man, Christ, through this repetition.

Cain – firstborn rejected
Abel – **second-born accepted**
Manasseh – firstborn bypassed
Ephraim – **second-born established**
Esau – firstborn ignored
Jacob – **second-born exalted**
Old Covenant – completed
New Covenant – **instituted**
Adam– "In Adam all die"   Christ – **In Christ all are made alive**

B. Recognition in Scripture

Sometimes a New Testament writer will identify an Old Testament type.

The Brasen Serpent – John 3:14
Manna – John 6:30-58
Melchisedec - Hebrews 7:1-3
The Tabernacle - Hebrews 9:16-24

The Gap Principle

I.   Identified by Christ Himself
II. Identified by Historical Evidence
III. Identified by the Character of God

chapter TWENTY-TWO

The Gap Principle

*And there was delivered unto him the book of
the prophet Esaias. And when he had opened
the book, he found the place where it was
written, The Spirit of the Lord is upon me,
because he hath anointed me to preach the
gospel to the poor; he hath sent me to heal the
brokenhearted, to preach deliverance to the
captives, and recovering of sight to the blind,
to set at liberty them that are bruised, To
preach the acceptable year of the Lord. And he
closed the book, and he gave it again to the
minister, and sat down. And the eyes of all
them that were in the synagogue were fastened
on him. And he began to say unto them, This
day is this scripture fulfilled in your ears.*
Luke 4:17-21

In simple terms the Gap Principle is that principle which identifies the fact that God ignores
certain periods of time, leaping over centuries
without comment.

There is some discussion about whether or not
this is a proper principle of Bible study. The argument usually centers around the first two verses in
Genesis, which we will deal with in this principle.
The principle is good, however. The problem
comes in the application of it. Of course, common
sense will tell you that the history of the world
could not be contained in one volume the size of

our Bible. The interesting thing to note is that sometimes these gaps will be in the middle of a verse.

I. Identified by Christ Himself

The strongest argument in favor of this principle is that Christ, Himself, recognized it. Luke records the event in chapter four of his gospel. Jesus was visiting a synagogue on the Sabbath day and was invited to read from the Scriptures. The Isaiah scroll was delivered to Him and He chose the place which we identify as Isaiah 61:1-2. When He reached the middle of verse two, He stopped.

The following verses are taken from the passage which Jesus was reading:

> *The Spirit of the Lord GOD is upon me; because the LORD hath anointed me to preach good tidings unto the meek; he hath sent me to bind up the brokenhearted, to proclaim liberty to the captives, and the opening of the prison to them that are bound;* *(2)* ***To proclaim the acceptable year of the LORD, and the day of vengeance of our God; to comfort all that mourn...***   Isaiah 61:1-2

The following verses are taken from Luke's recounting of the event:

> *And there was delivered unto him the book of the prophet Esaias. And when he had opened the book, he found the place where*

it was written, (18) The Spirit of the Lord is upon me, because he hath anointed me to preach the gospel to the poor; he hath sent me to heal the brokenhearted, to preach deliverance to the captives, and recovering of sight to the blind, to set at liberty them that are bruised, (19) **To preach the acceptable year of the Lord.** *(20) And he closed the book, and he gave it again to the minister, and sat down. And the eyes of all them that were in the synagogue were fastened on him. (21) And he began to say unto them, This day is this scripture fulfilled in your ears.*

Luke 4:17-20

Notice:

- Isaiah prophesies of the threefold work of the Messiah:
  1. To proclaim the acceptable year of the LORD
  2. To proclaim the day of vengeance of our God
  3. To comfort all that mourn
- Jesus says, in Luke's Gospel, that He is here to preach the acceptable year of the Lord, and then He stopped, leaving the other two works to be completed at a later date. The day of vengeance will be at the Second Advent. The day of comforting will follow that. We know of at least 2,000 years that fit in where the comma is in Isaiah 61:2.

II. Identified by Historical Evidence and Prophetical Revelation

A. The book of Revelation presents things from God's perspective. It does not necessarily follow chronological or consecutive order. The gap principle can definitely be applied in many passages. The following is one example:

> *(5)And she brought forth a man child, who was to rule all nations with a rod of iron: and her child was caught up unto God, and to his throne. (6) And the woman fled into the wilderness, where she hath a place prepared of God, that they should feed her there a thousand two hundred and threescore days.*   Revelation 12:5-6

Notice:
- The woman is Israel and the man child is Christ.
- Verse five tells of the ascension of Christ. Verse six tells of the tribulation. There are approximately 2,000 years between those verses.

B. The prophetical books are full of gaps in time. Often the prophet is speaking about a current event and at the same time he is foretelling something way into the future. In the following passage Isaiah is foretelling the birth of his own son, as well as the birth of Christ. There is an obvious gap between the birth of Christ and His acceptance of His governing responsibilities.

> *(6)For unto us a child is born, unto us a son is given: and the government shall be upon his shoulder: and his name shall be called Wonderful, Counsellor, The mighty God, The everlasting Father, The Prince of Peace. (7) Of the increase of his government and peace there shall be no end, upon the throne of David, and upon his kingdom, to order it, and to establish it with judgment and with justice from henceforth even for ever. The zeal of the LORD of hosts will perform this.* Isaiah 9:6-7

Notice:

- The Son is born, but the government is not yet on His shoulders.

III. Identified by the character of God

Some people have tried to link evolutionary theory with the gap between Genesis 1:1 and Genesis 1:2. This is a wrong premise. It has been suggested that dinosaurs roamed the earth between these two verses. This is also a wrong premise. It is simple to confirm that there were indeed dinosaurs at the time of the Great Flood. The Flood was the cause of the fossils that we are finding today (See II Peter 3:3-5.) Let's take an honest look, however, at the possibility of a gap between these two verses:

> **(1) In the beginning God created the heaven and the earth. (2) And the earth**

was without form, and void; and darkness was upon the face of the deep. And the Spirit of God moved upon the face of the waters. Genesis 1:1-2

A. The first thing to consider is that God did not create the heaven and earth in stages. Some have suggested that God created the earth without form and void and then shaped it later. However, David presents a different view. He states that the creation was not a process but, rather, it was a single event.

(6) **By the word of the LORD were the heavens made***; and all the host of them by the breath of his mouth. (7)He gathereth the waters of the sea together as an heap: he layeth up the depth in storehouses. (8)Let all the earth fear the LORD: let all the inhabitants of the world stand in awe of him. (9)For* **he spake, and it was done; he commanded, and it stood fast***.*   Psalm 33:6-9

B. Everything God created was good at the beginning. He did not create anything that was void of beauty.

...God saw the light, ...it was good Gen 1:4
...and God saw that it was good   Gen 1:10
...and God saw that it was good   Gen 1:12
...and God saw that it was good   Gen 1:18
...and God saw that it was good   Gen 1:21
...and God saw that it was good   Gen 1:25

And God saw every thing that he had made, and, behold, it was very good...   Gen 1:31

*For thus saith the LORD that created the heavens; God himself that formed the earth and made it; he hath established it, he created it not in **vain**, he formed it to be inhabited: I am the LORD; and there is none else.*

Isaiah 45:18

Notice:

- It is interesting to see that the word *vain* in Isaiah 45:18 is translated from the exact same word as void in Genesis 1:2.

C. Another thing to consider is that there is no "darkness" in God.

This then is the message which we have heard of him, and declare unto you, that God is light, and in him is no darkness at all.

I John 1:5

So what happened that caused the darkness in verse 2?

We really can only guess what might have happened. Putting together some facts that are mentioned in the Bible we can, however, make an educated guess.

- Satan's original condition was good – what happened when he fell?

(12) How art thou fallen from heaven, O Luci-fer, son of the morning! how art thou cut down to the ground, which didst weaken the nations! (13) For thou hast said in thine heart, I will ascend into heaven, I will exalt my throne above the stars of God: I will sit also upon the mount of the congregation, in the sides of the north: (14) I will ascend above the heights of the clouds; I will be like the most High. (15) Yet thou shalt be brought down to hell, to the sides of the pit. (16) They that see thee shall narrowly look upon thee, and consider thee, saying, Is this the man that made the earth to tremble, that did shake kingdoms; (17) That made the world as a wilderness, and destroyed the cities thereof; that opened not the house of his prisoners? Isaiah 14:12

There is obviously a double reference here as in the prophecy about the Prince of Persia, but it is clear that Satan fell from heaven and made a wreck when he did. Could that have been the pre-man earth?

- Here's something else to think about: Redemption was in the mind of God from the beginning of the creation of man.

(9) And to make all men see what is the fellow-ship of the mystery, which from the beginning of the world hath been hid in God, who created all things by Jesus Christ: (10) To the intent

that now unto the principalities and powers in heavenly places might be known by the church the manifold wisdom of God, (11) According to the eternal purpose which he purposed in Christ Jesus our Lord...

Ephesians 3: 9-11

Is there something bigger than "us" going on?

Notice: There are other verses as well that cause me to believe that the Gap Principle applies to Genesis 1:1 and Genesis 1:2. However, regardless of what you believe about its application, remember that the Gap Principle is important for Bible Study.

The Discrimination Principle

I.   The Second Coming of Christ and The Rapture of the Church
II. The Tribulation of the Saints and The Great Tribulation
III The Kingdom of Heaven and The Kingdom Age

chapter TWENTY-THREE

The Discrimination Principle

Study to shew thyself approved unto God,
a workman that needeth not to be ashamed,
rightly dividing the word of truth.
II Timothy 2:15

Sometimes there is confusion in Bible interpretation because there has been a confusion of key elements in a particular Bible Study. It is important for the Bible student to understand that there are some clear differences in certain Biblical elements. As the Apostle Paul admonishes Timothy, we should be diligent in the proper division or "discrimination" of such cases.

I. The Second Coming of Christ is different than the Rapture of the Church.

- Elements of The Second Coming of Christ
  He will come with His saints.
  Jude 14, Revelation 19:11-16

He will put His feet on earth.
Zechariah 14:4

- Elements of the Rapture
  The dead in Christ will be resurrected.
  I Thessalonians 4:13-16
  Believers who are alive will meet Him in
  the air.   I Thessalonians 4:17

II. The Tribulation of the Saints is different than the Great Tribulation.

- The Bible clearly teaches that the followers of Jesus will have tribulation. The perpetrator of this tribulation is the World. God is referred to as the Comforter in this case.
  John 16:33, Romans 5:3,
  I Thessalonians 3:4,
  II Corinthians 1:4, etc.

> *There are clear differences in certain Biblical Elements.*

- There will, however, be a time of Great Tribulation which will try the world. The perpetrator of the Great Tribulation is God. It is referred to as a portion of the Wrath of God.
  Matthew 24:21, Mark 13:24,
  Revelation 3:10, Revelation 14:7

Compare these verses:
Notice the phrase *the hour* in John 12:23 and Revelation 14:7.
See also Matthew 26:27, John 18:11, I Corin-

thians 11:25, Revelation 14:10, and Revelation 16:19. Notice the reference to "the cup." Jesus indicated that He would drink all of the cup of God's wrath for us. The cup of God's wrath is not only the Lake of Fire. It also includes the Great Tribulation.

III. The Kingdom of Heaven is different than the Kingdom Age.

- The Kingdom of Heaven is a spiritual Kingdom that is with us today.
  John 3:5, John 18:36, Luke 17:21,
  Matthew 16:28, Revelation 1:9

- The Kingdom Age will be a physical reign of Christ on this earth.
  Revelation 17:14, Revelation 19:16,
  II Samuel 7:10-13, Zechariah 6:13,
  Matthew 25:31, Luke 1:32, Jeremiah 3:17

Appendix A

The Christo-centric principle of Bible study is touched on in the Unity Principle. It is based on the same concept as the Unity Principle; therefore, the author did not feel that it was necessary to repeat it in a chapter of its own. However, there are some things that can be added to the study of this principle.

Here is a listing of how you can see Jesus, the hero of His-story (history), in the Old Testament.

Genesis ----------------- Creator
Exodus ------------- Redeemer
Leviticus --------- Law Keeper
Numbers ---------- Tabernacle
Deuteronomy ---- 2nd Chance
Joshua -------------- Conqueror
Judges -------------------- Judge
Ruth -------------- Bridegroom
Samuel --------- Lord of Lords
Kings ---------- King of Kings
Chronicles ----- Lion of Judah
Ezra -------------- Word of God
Nehemiah ----------- Rebuilder
Esther ------------ God of Israel
Job --------------------- Sufferer
Psalms --------- Song of Songs
Proverbs --------------- Wisdom
Ecclesiastes ------------ Servant
Canticles ----------------- Lover
Isaiah ----------------- Sacrifice

Jeremiah----------- Proclaimer
Lamentations -- Broken Heart
Ezekiel ------------- Revivalist
Daniel ---------- Prince of God
Hosea ----------------- Husband
Joel ----- Blessing of the Spirit
Amos ----------- Average Man
Obadiah ------- Sceptered One
Jonah-------------- Resurrected
Micah ---- Ruler of Bethlehem
Nahum--------- Burdened One
Habakkuk ---- Righteous Gov.
Zephaniah ------------ Chastiser
Haggai ------------------ Restorer
Zechariah --------- The Branch
Malachi-------------- Deliverer

Appendix B

The following is a complete listing of every time the word εκλεσια is used in the Textus Receptus, and how it has been translated into the Authorized Version of the English Bible. The author has also included here his opinion on whether or not each verse is a reference to a local organization or a larger organism.

DEFINING VERSES

Reference   Translation

Reference	Translation
Acts 7:38	Church in the Wilderness
Acts 19:32	Assembly
Acts 19:39	Assembly
Acts 19:41	Assembly

It is interesting to note the two directions in which this word was used when not referring to the church as we know it. In the Acts 7:38 reference the word is emphasizing the separation from the world. They are called out to an ambiguous place, the wilderness. This demonstrates that the word church can refer to an organism which is not in a specific location. A direct reference to the Kingdom of God called out of darkness.

The next three references are translated "Assembly." This refers to a specific location where individuals have gathered together. This is how the word church is used most of the time in the Bible, and is a direct reference to the organization we call the local church.

THE ORGANISM OF THE CHURCH

Matthew 16:18	Ephesians 1:22	Ephesians 5:32
Acts 5:11	Ephesians 3:10	Philippians 3:6
Acts 12:1	Ephesians 3:21	Colossians 1:18
Acts 20:28	Ephesians 5:23	Colossians 1:24
I Corinthians 10:32	Ephesians 5:24	Hebrews 2:12
I Corinthians 11:22	Ephesians 5:25	Hebrews 12:23
I Corinthians 12:28	Ephesians 5:27	
Galatians 1:13	Ephesians 5:29	

THE ORGANIZATION OF THE CHURCH

Matthew 18:17	I Corinthians 6:4	II Corinthians 11:28
Acts 8:1	I Corinthians 7:17	II Corinthians 12:13
Acts 8:3	I Corinthians 11:16	Galatians 1:2
Acts 9:31	I Corinthians 11:18	Galatians 1:22
Acts 11:22	I Corinthians 14:4	Philippians 4:15
Acts 11:26	I Corinthians 14:5	Colossians 4:15
Acts 12:5	I Corinthians 14:12	Colossians 4:16
Acts 13:1	I Corinthians 14:19	I Thessalonians 1:1
Acts 14:23	I Corinthians 14:23	I Thessalonians 2:14
Acts 14:27	I Corinthians 14:28	II Thessalonians 1:1
Acts 15:3	I Corinthians 14:33	II Thessalonians 1:4
Acts 15:4	I Corinthians 14:34	I Timothy 3:5
Acts 15:22	I Corinthians 14:35	I Timothy 5:16
Acts 15:41	I Corinthians 16:1	Philemon 2
Acts 16:5	I Corinthians 16:19	James 5:14
Acts 18:22	I Corinthians 16:19	I Peter 5:13
Acts 20:17	II Corinthians 1:1	III John 6
Romans 16:1	II Corinthians 8:1	III John 9
Romans 16:4	II Corinthians 8:18	III John 10
Romans 16:16	II Corinthians 8:19	Revelation 1:4
Romans 16:23	II Corinthians 8:23	Revelation 1:11
I Corinthians 1:2	II Corinthians 8:24	Revelation 1:20
I Corinthians 4:17	II Corinthians 11:8	Revelation 1:20

THE ORGANIZATION Continued

Revelation 2:7	Revelation 2:23	Revelation 3:13
Revelation 2:11	Revelation 2:29	Revelation 3:22
Revelation 2:17	Revelation 3:6	Revelation 22:16

THE ORGANISM AND THE ORGANIZATION

The following list can be taken either way or both ways according to the author's opinion.

Acts 2:47	Revelation 2:12
I Corinthians 15:9	Revelation 2:18
I Timothy 3:15	Revelation 3:1
Revelation 2:1	Revelation 3:7
Revelation 2:8	Revelation 3:14

Appendix C

The following is a list of the seven different dispensations identified by the kind of government that God used in each period. Notice that in three different dispensations the Lord chose to give us the freedom of choice.

1– Innocence - A Theocratical Government
During the dispensation of Innocence God was the only Authority. This is called a Theocracy.

2– Conscience – Personal Responsibility
The dispensation of conscience found man somewhat on his own. He was guided only by his newly acquired conscience, which came from eating of the tree of the knowledge of good and evil.

3– Government – A Patriarchal Government
In this dispensation God gave specific direction to man to judge other men. "Whoso sheddeth man's blood, by man shall his blood be shed." Genesis 9:6

4– Promise – Personal Responsibility
In the dispensation of Promise we once again find man bound by a personal covenant with

God. This covenant is meant to direct his life.

5– Law – A Constitutional Government

The written law which God intended man to follow explicitly is obviously a constitutional form of government.

6– Grace – Personal Responsibility

Grace gives individuals room to grow and change. Man is personally responsible to follow the leading and teachings of the Holy Spirit.

7– Kingdom – A Dictatorial Government

The kingdom age is not a true Theocracy because God shares power with his saints. However, it is ruled by the will of One and sentence is carried out with an iron hand.

Appendix D

The Jewish Wedding Ceremony
by Rabbi Mordechai Becher

In traditional Jewish literature marriage is actually called *kiddushin*, which translates as "sanctification" or "dedication." "Sanctification," indicates that what is happening is not just a social arrangement or contractual agreement, but a spiritual bonding and the fulfillment of a *mitzvah*, a Divine precept. "Dedication," indicates that the couple now have an exclusive relationship, that involves total dedication of the bride and groom to each other, to the extent of them becoming, as the Kabbalists state, "one soul in two bodies."

shidduch
The very first stage of a traditional Jewish marriage, is the *shidduch*, or matchmaking. This means that the process of finding a partner is not haphazard or based on purely external aspects. Rather, a close friend or relative of the young man or woman, who knows someone that they feel may be a compatible partner, suggests that they meet. The purpose of the meeting is for the prospective bride and groom to determine if they are indeed compatible. The meetings usually focus on discussion of issues important to marriage as well as casual conversation. The Talmud states that the couple must also be physically attractive to each other, something that can only be determined by meeting. According to Jewish law physical contact is not allowed between a man and a woman until they are married (except for certain close relatives), and also they may not be alone together in a closed room or secluded area. This helps to ensure that one's choice of partner will be

based on the intellect and emotion as opposed to physical desire alone.

vort - engagement
When the families have met, and the young couple have decided to marry, the families usually announce the occasion with a small reception, known as a *vort.* Some families sign a contract, the *tenaim,* meaning "conditions," that delineates the obligations of each side regarding the wedding and a final date for the wedding. Others do this at the wedding reception an hour or so before the marriage. One week before the wedding the bride and groom, the *chosson* and *kallah,* stop seeing each other, in order to enhance the joy of their wedding through their separation.

ketuvah
At the reception itself, the first thing usually done is the completion, signing and witnessing of the *ketuvah,* or marriage contract. This contract is ordained by Mishnaic law (circa 170 CE) and according to some authorities dates back to Biblical times. The *ketuvah,* written in Aramaic, details the husband's obligations to his wife: food, clothing, dwelling and pleasure. It also creates a lien on all his property to pay her a sum of money and support should he divorce her, or predecease her. The document is signed by the groom and witnessed by two people, and has the standing of a legally binding agreement, that in many countries is enforceable by secular law. The *ketuvah* is often written as an illuminated manuscript, and becomes a work of art in itself, and many couples frame it and display it in their home.

bedekin
After the signing of the *ketuvah,* which is usually accompanied by some light snacks and some hard liquor for the traditional *lechaims* (the Jewish salute when drinking, which means, "to life!"), the groom does the *bedekin,* or "veiling." The groom, together with his father and future father-in-law, is accompanied by musicians and the male guests to the room where the bride is receiving her guests. She sits, like a

queen, on a throne-like chair surrounded by her family and friends. The groom, who has not seen her for a week (an eternity for a young couple!), covers her face with her veil. This ceremony is mainly for the legal purpose of the groom identifying the bride before the wedding.

chuppah

The next stage is known as the *chuppah,* or "canopy." The *chuppah* is a decorated piece of cloth held aloft as a symbolic home for the new couple. It is usually held outside, under the stars, as a sign of the blessing given by G-d to the patriarch Abraham, that his children shall be "as the stars of the heavens." The groom is accompanied to the *chuppah* by his parents, and usually wears a white robe, known as a *kittel,* to indicate the fact that for the bride and groom, life is starting anew with a clean white slate, since they are uniting to become a new entity, without past sins. In fact, the bride and groom usually fast on the day of the wedding (until the *chuppah*) since for them it is like *Yom Kippur,* the Day of Atonement. While the bride comes to the *chuppah* with her parents, a cantor sings a selection from the Song of Songs, and the groom prays that his unmarried friends find their true partners in life.

When the bride arrives at the *chuppah* she circles the groom seven times with her mother and future mother-in-law, while the groom continues to pray. This symbolizes the idea of the woman being a protective, surrounding light of the household, that illuminates it with understanding and love from within and protects it from harm from the outside. The number seven parallels the seven days of creation, and symbolizes the fact that the bride and groom are about to create their own "new world" together.

Under the chuppah, an honored Rabbi or family member then recites a blessing over wine, and a blessing that praises and thanks G-d for giving us laws of sanctity and morality to preserve the sanctity of family life and of the Jewish people. The bride and groom then drink from the wine. The blessings are recited over wine, since wine is symbolic of life: it begins as grape-juice, goes through fermentation, during which it is sour, but in the end turns into a superior product that brings joy, and has a wonderful taste. The full cup of wine also symbolizes the overflowing of Divine blessing, as in the verse in Psalms, "My cup runneth over."

Kiddushin

The groom, now takes a plain gold ring and places it on the finger of the bride, and recites in the presence of two witnesses, "Behold you are sanctified (betrothed) to me with this ring, according to the Law of Moses and Israel." The ring symbolizes the concept of the groom encompassing, protecting and providing for his wife. The *ketuvah* is now read aloud, usually by another honoree, after which it is given to the bride.

sheva brachos

After this, the *sheva brachos,* or seven blessings, are recited, either by one Rabbi, or at many weddings a different blessing is given to various people the families wish to honor. The blessings are also recited over a full cup of wine. The blessings begin with praising G-d for His creation in general and creation of the human being and proceed with praise for the creation of the human as a "two part creature," woman and man. The blessings express the hope that the new couple will rejoice together forever as though they are the original couple, Adam and Eve in the Garden of Eden. The blessings also include a prayer that Jerusalem will be fully rebuilt and restored with the Temple in its midst and the Jewish people within her gates.

At this point the couple again share in drinking the cup of wine, and the groom breaks a glass by stamping on it. This custom dates back to Talmudic times, and symbolizes the idea of our keeping Jerusalem and Israel in our minds even at times of our joy. Just as the Temple in Jerusalem is destroyed, so we break a utensil to show our identification with the sorrow of Jewish exile. The verse, "If I forget thee O' Jerusalem, let my right hand forget its cunning: If I do not raise thee over my own joy, let my tongue cleave to the roof of my mouth", is sometimes recited at this point. With the breaking of the glass the band plays, and the guests usually break out into dancing and cries of "*Mazaltov! Mazaltov!*" (Some say, tongue in cheek, that this moment symbolizes the last time the groom gets to "put his foot down")

cheder yichud

Now that the couple are married they are accompanied by dancing guests to the *cheder yichud,* "the room of privacy." They may now be alone in a closed room together, an intimacy reserved only for a married couple. In fact, according to many Jewish legal authorities, the very fact that they are alone together in a locked room, is a requirement of the legal act of marriage, and hence their entry into the room must be observed by the two witnesses of the marriage.

While the bride and groom are alone together (usually eating, after having fasted all day) the guests sit down to eat a festive meal. The meal is preceded by ritual washing of the hands, and the blessing over bread. At some point, the band announces the arrival "for the very first time, Mr. and Mrs. _____!!!" and everyone joins in dancing around the bride and groom. The dancing, in accordance with Jewish law requires a separation between men and women for reasons of modesty, and hence there is a *mechitzah*, or partition between the men and women. The main focus of the dancing is to entertain and enhance the joy of the newlyweds, hence large circles are formed around the "king and queen," and different guests often perform in front of the seated couple. It is not unusual to see jugglers, fire eaters, and acrobats at a wedding (most of whom are guests, not professionals!) The meal ends with the *Birchas Hamazon*, Grace After Meals, and again the seven blessings are recited over wine, shared afterwards by the bride and groom.

Appendix E

In Revelation chapter four and five we are introduced to the throne room of the Almighty immediately following the rapture of the church. A book is presented which has seven seals on it. John weeps because no one can open the seals, which indicates that the contents of the book are important to him. No one is able to open the seals except for One who looks like a Lion and a Lamb. There is no question that this Person is Jesus Christ, the Son of God and the Second person of the Trinity.

When one considers the fact that Jesus Christ is our Advocate before the throne, and that, when the seals are opened, there is great rejoicing about Salvation, one wonders if, in fact, the book contains information pertinent to our salvation.

A closer look at the seven seals reveals an interesting similarity to the seven dispensations in which God dealt with man in different ways, as the truth of His mercy and grace was carefully and masterfully revealed. Could the unlocking of the seals of the book by the Lamb actually be the telling of the story of man and his redemption? Consider these things:

Seal 1—White Horse– The dispensation of Innocence
Rev 6:2 And I saw, and behold a white horse: and he that sat on him had a bow; and a crown was given unto him: and he went forth conquering, and to conquer.
White is always a symbol of purity and innocence. Adam and Noah were given the specific command to rule and subdue the earth. The horse indicates a continual movement on the earth. While the dispensation of Innocence progressed to another dispensation still every child begins with Innocence and opportunity.

Seal 2—Red Horse– The dispensation of Conscience

Rev 6:4 And there went out another horse that was red: and power was given to him that sat thereon to take peace from the earth, and that they should kill one another: and there was given unto him a great sword.

When Cain killed Abel he began a period of killing and destruction on our earth that has never been changed. While man is now responsible to live according to his understanding of the difference between good and evil (his conscience), he continually fails and is affected by the trampling of the red horse.

Seal 3- Black Horse– The dispensation of Government

Rev 6:5-6 And when he had opened the third seal, I heard the third beast say, Come and see. And I beheld, and lo a black horse; and he that sat on him had a pair of balances in his hand. And I heard a voice in the midst of the four beasts say, A measure of wheat for a penny, and three measures of barley for a penny; and see thou hurt not the oil and the wine.

Several times throughout the Old Testament we find the weights and measures mentioned. Daniel 5:27 is the most clear and most quoted example of the balances. It is a reference to the Supreme Judge making judgment calls on the actions of men. Verse six speaks of the bounty that God gives to man to see what he will do with it. It is not a reference to a famine (See II Kings 7:1-2 for an example).

Seal 4– Pale Horse– The dispensation of Promise

Rev 6:8 And I looked, and behold a pale horse: and his name that sat on him was Death, and Hell followed with him. And power was given unto them over the fourth part of the earth, to kill with sword, and with hunger, and with death, and with the beasts of the earth.

The Pale horse declares all condemned that the righteousness by faith may be established. This horse reflects the truth that is spelled out in Romans 6:23, "For the wages of sin is death; but the gift of God is eternal life through Jesus Christ our Lord."

Seal 5– Souls under the Altar-dispensation of Law

Rev 6:9-11 And when he had opened the fifth seal, I saw under the altar the souls of them that were slain for the word of God, and for the testimony which they held: And they cried with a loud voice, saying, How long, O Lord, holy and true, dost thou not judge and avenge our blood on them that dwell on the earth? And white robes were given unto every one of them; and it was said unto them, that they should rest yet for a little season, until their fellowservants also and their brethren, that should be killed as they were, should be fulfilled.

This must be a reference to Old Testament saints who are not complete without us (Hebrews11:39). Notice the cry for vengeance, which is a very Old Testament cry. The book of Psalms is full of this concept, as well as, every one of the prophets. These saints are under the altar waiting. Could this be a reference to those in Abraham's bosom mentioned by the Lord, himself, in Luke 16:19-31? These are the ones who escaped the 4th horse by faith (Romans 4).

Seal 6– Sealed Saints– dispensation of Grace

Rev 6:12-17 And I beheld when he had opened the sixth seal, and, lo, there was a great earthquake; and the sun became black as sackcloth of hair, and the moon became as blood; And the stars of heaven fell unto the earth, even as a fig tree casteth her untimely figs, when she is shaken of a mighty wind. And the heaven departed as a scroll when it is rolled together; and every mountain and island were moved out of their places. And the kings of the earth, and the great men, and the rich men, and the chief captains, and the mighty men, and every bondman, and every free man, hid themselves in the dens and in the rocks of the mountains; And said to the mountains and rocks, Fall on us, and hide us from the face of him that sitteth on the throne, and from the wrath of the Lamb: For the great day of his wrath is come; and who shall be able to stand?

Immediately following the sixth seal chapter seven follows with an extensive description of a seal placed on the servants of God. When this seal is placed no one is calling for vengeance. Instead the songs are about salvation and the Lamb, who has not been mentioned in the first five seals.

Take a step back and look at the sixth seal as the heavenly view of the Crucifixion when the King of the Universe was hanging on the cross. Think about the universal shaking that must have happened when God gave Himself for our sins. One particular identifying mark is the moon which turned to blood. This was prophesied by the prophet Joel and repeated by Peter at Pentecost indicating that the people in the crowd had witnessed the moon turned to blood. Jesus prophesied that after the tribulation the moon would be darkened not turned to blood (Matthew 24:29).

Seal 7–The Tribulation–dispensation of the Kingdom

Rev 8:1 And when he had opened the seventh seal, there was silence in heaven about the space of half an hour.

When the seventh seal is opened there is a shift in the dialogue. No longer are we talking of the past. Now we are watching the story unfold in front of us. This goes from chapter eight to chapter twenty. We see Babylon completely decimated in the same way that God completely destroyed Egypt during the Exodus. Here the King of Kings shows us in detail from four different angles the compete destruction of the Mystery Babylon—the worlds government system—and the subsequent establishment of the Kingdom of Christ on the earth.

References

Archaic Words, Vance, Laurence M.

A Short Intro. to the Lit. of the Bible, Moulton, Richard

Baker's Bible Atlas, Pfeiffer, Charles F.

Commentary on the Old Testament, Keil, C.F.-Delitzch, F.

Clarke's Commentary, Clarke, Adam

Daniel & Revelation Made Plain, Cambron, Mark G.

Dictionary of Bible Manners and Customs, Deursen, A. Van

Dispensational Truth, Larkin, Clarence

Final Authority, Grady, William P.

Gleanings in Genesis, Pink, Arthur W.

Hermeneutics, Haifley, David R.

Hermeneutics, Virkler, Henry A.

Jesus is Coming, Blackstone, W.E.

Manners and Customs of Bible Lands, Wight, Fred H.

Mastered by the Bible, Cambron, Mark G.

Synthetic Bible Studies, Gray, James M.

The Biblical Trace of the Church, Schell, W.G.

The Genesis Flood, Whitcomb, John - Morris, Henry

The Language of the King James Bible, Riplinger, Gail

The Life and Times of Jesus the Messiah, Edersheim, Alfred

The Superhuman Origin of The Bible, Rogers, Henry

Treasures from the Tenach, Duff-Forbes, L.W.G.

Other Books by the same author available on www.amazon.com

- **Reaching your community for Christ**

- **P.K. Problems**

- **Tactical Advantages**

- **Practical Advantages**

- **Does God Care What you Wear?**

- **How to Start a Local Church Bible Institute**

www.mbcmattoon.com

Printed in Great Britain
by Amazon

59398552R00119